RESOURCE BOOKS FOR TEACHERS

series editor

ALAN MALEY

CREATING STORIES WITH CHILDREN

Andrew Wright

Oxford University Press 1997

Oxford University Press
Great Clarendon Street, Oxford OX2 6DP

Oxford   New York
Athens   Auckland   Bangkok   Bogota   Bombay
Buenos Aires   Calcutta   Cape Town   Dar es Salaam
Delhi   Florence   Hong Kong   Istanbul   Karachi
Kuala Lumpur   Madras   Madrid   Melbourne
Mexico City   Nairobi   Paris   Singapore
Taipei   Tokyo   Toronto

and associated companies in
Berlin   Ibadan

Oxford and *Oxford English*
are trade marks of Oxford University Press

ISBN 0 19 437204 9

© Oxford University Press 1997

Typeset by Wyvern Typesetting Ltd, Bristol

Printed in Hong Kong

Acknowledgements

I would like to thank the following people:

All the children and teachers I have worked with over the years.

Eva Benkö for her suggestions and classroom experience incorporated into this book.

Cynthia Beresford, John Morgan, Mario Rinvolucri, and Jim Wingate for their constantly refreshing energy and ideas and many practical suggestions.

David Betteridge, who has been an inspiration, a guide, and an 'ear' for all my stories.

Julia Dudás for her constant support, teaching experience, and specific ideas incorporated into this book.

Dorothy Heathcote has been a major influence on my work in oral story-making with children (see Further Reading).

Erich Krassnitzer for organizing so many visits to so many schools.

Alan Maley for his invitation to contribute to the series but also for his rich guidance through his own published work, in particular *Drama Techniques in Language Learning*.

Irmgard Meyer for being the first person to encourage, support, and advise me in my storytelling and story-making for children.

Duncan Williamson for my being able to meet and listen to one of the world's greatest storytellers.

I have learnt a great deal from working with Word and Action (Dorset).

Illustrations by Andrew Wright © Oxford University Press.

To my children: Tom, Katy, Timea, and Alexandra

Contents

The author and series editor

Andrew Wright is an author, illustrator, teacher trainer, and storyteller. He has written a number of books for teachers including the companion book to this one, *Storytelling with Children*, also in this series; *Games for Language Learning, 1000+ Pictures for Teachers to Copy*, and *Five Minute Activities* (with Penny Ur). He has also written *Spellbinders*, a series of six books for children at three levels for Oxford University Press. He has worked in thirty countries as a teacher trainer, always concentrating on the application of practical and enjoyable activities in the classroom. In recent years he has worked with about 25,000 students as a storyteller and story-maker. Ten of his stories have been recorded by the BBC World Service, and ten have been broadcast on German Television and Thames Television in Britain.

Alan Maley worked for The British Council from 1962 to 1988, serving as English Language Officer in Yugoslavia, Ghana, Italy, France, and China, and as Regional Representative in South India (Madras). From 1988 to 1993 he was Director-General of the Bell Educational Trust, Cambridge. He is currently Senior Fellow in the Department of English Language and Literature of the National University of Singapore. He has written *Literature*, in this series, *Beyond Words, Sounds Interesting, Sounds Intriguing, Words, Variations on a Theme*, and *Drama Techniques in Language Learning* (all with Alan Duff), *The Mind's Eye* (with Françoise Grellet and Alan Duff), and *Learning to Listen* and *Poem into Poem* (with Sandra Moulding). He is also Series Editor for the New Perspectives and Oxford Supplementary Skills series.

Foreword

The success of Andrew Wright's companion volume in this series, *Storytelling with Children*, testifies to the re-awakening of interest in stories as a resource for language learning. But, whereas *Storytelling with Children* drew upon stories 'out there', *Creating Stories with Children* is grounded in children's ability to create their own stories from 'in here'.

The book is based on a passionate belief in the creative capacity of children provided they are given encouragement and appropriate guidance. The activities have been carefully devised to give maximum encouragement to children within a structured framework, thereby building confidence in their own creative output. The author emphasizes (and demonstrates) that creative story-making can be done even with children whose English is minimal.

Many teachers share these beliefs but have been somewhat at a loss as to how to get started. This book attempts to provide practical support for such teachers. In it you will find a set of materials leading progressively from warm-up activities through the retelling of familiar stories to fully-fledged independent creations.

A key component in motivating children is the possibility of publishing their work. In Chapter 8, 'Making books', Andrew Wright draws on his extensive experience as an artist and a teacher of art to offer a set of highly original ideas for publishing children's stories.

The activities and the friendly, helpful manner in which they are presented are a breath of fresh air in the sometimes fusty corridors of methodology. It is impossible not to be infected by the author's enthusiasm and by his belief in the creative capacity of children.

Alan Maley

Introduction

It is important for children to make stories as well as to receive and to respond to stories from other people. When we make stories we take our experience and make it meaningful for ourselves rather than waiting for other people to do it for us. When children create and tell a story in the foreign language the story and the language become theirs.

This book is a sequel to *Storytelling with Children* (OUP, 1995) which contains activities and advice on helping children to respond actively to stories. This book takes them further, helping them to create their own stories and make the English language their own.

Who is this book for?

Children

The activities in this book are aimed at children between the ages of four and fourteen, with the majority being appropriate for children from about ten who are learning English as a foreign or second language.

Some of the activities can be done by near beginners (in their first year of English) but the majority require at least a year of English (elementary and above).

There is a written component in many of the activities, but you can omit this in most cases if it is too difficult for your children or if you prefer to concentrate on oral English, and substitute a spoken or 'performed' outcome.

Teachers

This book is for teachers who:

- believe that stories are a necessary part of a child's day and not just an occasional luxury

- want to help their children to become willing and able to use their limited amount of the foreign language to tell stories

- believe in encouraging fluency, and that making mistakes is an essential characteristic of the way a child learns and develops (avoiding mistakes means, to a significant extent, avoiding learning).

Children creating stories in a foreign language

Children respond to your purpose

If the teacher's main motives are to help the children to enjoy making stories and to be willing to try to use their limited amount of the foreign language creatively, then the children will respond to this. However, story-making in the foreign language classroom (and indeed, often, the mother tongue classroom) has often been aimed purely at testing the learner's understanding of the rules of grammar and his or her knowledge of vocabulary. If testing is the chief motive of the main reader of his or her work, then the child will soon learn to concentrate on avoiding mistakes rather than on trying to use the language.

When my son was eleven and just starting secondary school in England he wrote a story entitled 'The End of the World', in five lines. The teacher had written underneath, 'Five spelling mistakes. Correct them.' I said, 'Tom, you have managed to bring about the end of the world in five lines. Congratulations.' He replied, 'There's something you learn at school. The less you do, the less mistakes you can make.' What a tragic position for a child to take at such a point in his education!

The importance of creativity

Creativity is important in language teaching because:

- language teaching, particularly of children, is about the development of the whole person and not just one minor aspect. Creativity, a key part of the child's development, is enriching for the individual and for society
- some learners cannot apply their full intelligence if they are not given the opportunity and encouragement to be creative with the 'new' language, even in their first week of learning it.
- by 'playing' with the language children make it their own
- some learners need to experience a rich flow of the language in order to 'feel' the character of each word.

Fluency and accuracy

Fluency is an important aspect of creativity. Fluency means, essentially, the willingness to 'have a go' with the language you have, whether it is in speaking and writing or listening and reading. It takes time to develop and it depends on you, the teacher, giving it time and purpose and emphasizing how important it is.

Of course we need accuracy. However, accuracy and fluency need not be in conflict. Interesting and relevant ideas need to be clearly expressed, and correct grammar, spelling, and punctuation are part of this.

But my children don't have enough language

Timea! Where's Timea?
Is she here? No!
Is she here? No!
Is she here? No!
Oh, Timea! There you are!

That is a story with perfect, completed sentences.

Big ... dog ... small ... cat ... run ... jump ... tree.

Here a list of single words tells the story, but the story is creative and fluent in the ideas conveyed.

These are stories made with almost no language, but they engage you. You want to hear what happens! They have a beginning, a problem, an emotion, an action, and an end.

Most of the activities in this book can only be done by the children if you allow them to use very simple or incomplete sentences (or even lists of single words), particularly in their first draft or contribution.

Here are some practical suggestions:

- encourage any contribution
- don't ask the children to think consciously about accuracy when they are thinking creatively
- do a lot of preparation as a class before asking the children to work on their own
- do a lot of *oral* story-making before moving into written story making—both in terms of children's overall development, but also within each activity
- write a lot of useful words and phrases on the board
- extend the copying or minor adaptation phase (see Chapter 3), giving reassurance but a feeling of creativity
- rejoice in their willingness to contribute
- let story making be a frequent activity rather than an occasional one
- let other art forms or media enrich the presentation so that the effect is not one of a limited vocabulary at all! E-mail, books, scrolls, crazy books, and posters can be used to heighten and enrich a written story. Music, mime, masks, the overhead projector, and the audio and video tape recorder can be used to enrich the spoken form.

Imaginary stories and real experiences

It is much easier to invent a totally imaginary story with limited language than it is to describe real experiences. When you *invent* a story you can use the words you have got. Activities leading to imaginary stories form the majority of this book because it is easier for the children to achieve something. But stories based on the child's own experience are equally important.

Writing

When to introduce writing, particularly writing in English with its irregular sound/spelling relationship, is contentious and beyond the scope of this book. I would suggest that you follow your present policy on the introduction of writing and adapt the activities given here to that policy.

However, I would argue that the discussion above on creativity, fluency, and accuracy is relevant to writing in second language learning as well as in mother tongue development. In general, move from oral to written story-making, and from fluency to accuracy.

Process writing

This is the term applied to the idea of emphasizing the whole craft of writing rather than the production of mistake-free texts for the teacher. Emphasis is on the process of:

- researching the subject and the intended reader
- drafting first ideas
- trying the first draft out
- redrafting
- trying out the second draft
- drafting the final version
- publishing i.e. making the text available.

In principle I think it is a good idea. However, there is a danger that we will bore children if we make them go through all these steps every time.

You will find suggestions for more than one draft in many of the activities in this book. That is because there is often a very real public outlet for the finished object. The idea of publishing is the most important part of the process writing idea—it gives children a reason for doing a good job which matters to them.

Publishing

Traditionally, the only person who read what children wrote was the teacher. Now we know how important it is to try to make the children's writing widely available, as often as possible. Publishing can be through e-mail, books, posters, or cards, which are read by other children in the class, used in other classes, put in the school library, exhibited at the school or in a local library or bookshop, or broadcast world wide. Stories in the form of dramatic productions can be performed for other groups in the class, for other classes, or for an end-of-term show for parents. Stories can also be put on audio and video tape.

Your work will still involve reading through what the children write and working out how to help them to improve their understanding and control of the language. However, you will not be seen as the *reason* for writing, but as someone who is trying to help them to write better in general. For ideas on making books, see Chapter 8.

Evaluation, marking, and correcting

Correcting writing is one way of trying to help someone to learn. It is probably not a very efficient way of doing so! This is an unconventional assertion when you think of the number of hours spent by language teachers all over the world correcting written work in the middle of the night. Correcting is not enough if it is not related to what the child is trying to achieve.

Here are some suggestions for responding to a child's stories:

1 Let the children know, before they begin, what your real motives are in getting them to write. Then keep to that agreement. If you want to test their accuracy above all, then tell them so. There is nothing dishonourable in that. But if you tell them, with a look of excitement, that you want them to write a story about the end of the world and then merely pick out five spelling mistakes, you will build up an element of mistrust.

2 If you want everything: creativity, the development of fluency, and accuracy, then create a situation in which that is natural. For example, if a book is to be made and put in the school library, it must obviously be interesting and accurate! The first draft is motivated by interest and the second draft gives more emphasis to accuracy.

Respond to the first draft by commenting on:

– freshness of the main ideas
– clarity and expression
– main sequencing for excitement and sense
– how well the story grips the reader's interest
– richness of detail (using descriptions that appeal to several senses)
– richness of the 'sound' of the language.

Respond to the second draft by commenting on:

– grammar
– syntax
– punctuation
– spelling.

A particular technique is to tell the children that you want them to write a story. Tell them they are going to work on the story twice.

First time: they write as much as they like and you will only read it for interest and clarity.

Second time: they will work on the first 100 words and make that section of text as accurate as possible. You will mark it in the old-fashioned way for accuracy.

3 You will inevitably do some marking. Ideally you would do it sitting alongside the child, but this is usually not possible, as you are too busy. For marking to be effective in helping the children to develop their understanding, it has to be more than just red pen all over their work.

If you use underlining and symbols in the margin, the children must be familiar with what these mean. You might build up familiarity by correcting texts on the board with the class as a whole, first of all getting the children to hypothesize about the mistakes and then getting them to underline and use the symbols.

4 Regard the mistakes you find in the children's work as your mistakes as much as theirs—the mistakes are a sign that you have not managed to help the children to master those language points! What matters is not correction of that error at that moment, but that the child learns not to do it in future. It might often be better not to correct the error but to make a mental note that you must find activities to focus the child's mind on that language feature at some future time.

5 Ask a child to read his or her story to someone else. The listener should have a task connected with the text. If the reader finds it difficult to read his or her own work and if the listener cannot do the task, then the reader might realize that what they have written is not correct.

6 Ask one child to read another child's story back to them. If the writer realizes that the other child cannot read his or her handwriting it might be helpful feedback. If some phrases sound clumsy, it might raise questions in the writer's mind, even if there are no precise answers. One of the most important things for a child to grasp is that writing is normally for other people to read, and that therefore the writer is responsible for communicating clearly.

7 In the early stages, work on a child's work with the class as a whole (providing it is acceptable to the child). For example, the child might have written, 'The man walks in the wood.' You could ask the class, 'Is the man old or young, big or small? How does he walk? What is the wood like?'

8 Ask groups or pairs to work on each others' writing, underlining what they think is wrong and looking up spellings in a dictionary.

How to use this book

How this book is organized

1 Story warmers

The activities in this section are for helping the children to get into a story-making frame of mind.

2 The craft of story-making

The children experiment with some of the features of good story-making—particularizing details, bubbling and clustering ideas, looking at desires and their associated difficulties, planning and sequencing. The final part of this section is 'Stories from personal experience'.

3 Retelling

In this kind of story-making the children retell a story, transforming it by changes of content, medium, or style.

4 Beginnings and endings

The children have one part of a story—first, last, or middle, and complete it or continue it and pass it on.

5 Filling in and filling out

A sequence of different bits of information is used to stimulate and to guide the children in making their story. The bits of information can be of any kind, and can be received through any of the senses.

6 Sorting and sequencing

Children have lots of different bits of information to sort out and put into a sequence to tell a story.

7 Starting with one thing

One bit of information is used to stimulate and guide the children into their story-making.

8 Making books

Different ways of making books can encourage creativity, as well as helping children to present their work neatly. The way we choose to present and tell a story affects the content and the style of telling.

Further reading

A brief, annotated list of publications which you might like to follow up.

How each activity is organized

Level

The level given is only an approximation. A slight change to the activity can make it much less or much more demanding. If your children have not started writing yet, leave out the writing aspect of the activity. If they have not started using a past tense form, use a present tense form. If you play a bigger role in the activity, giving more language, writing useful words and phrases on the board, or doing brief practice activities, you can help lower-proficiency children do the same activity.

The levels given in this book are as follows:

Beginners
This category ranges from children with little or no knowledge of English to those who have been learning it for about a year. Their active use of the language will be very limited and they may not be able to make full sentences (see page 3 'But my children don't have enough language').

Elementary
These children are able to use English more actively, and to make simple sentences and questions. They will have a wider range of vocabulary.

Pre-intermediate
These children will be more capable of recognizing sentence patterns and more willing to 'have a go' at generating language of their own. They are ready to learn structures such as the past simple and comparatives, and functions such as obligation, requests, or making suggestions.

Language

Only the key language focus can be shown. All of the activities are designed to practise language already taught, rather than to present language items for the first time.

Time

A rough guide only. Take into account that you can often do half the activity quite satisfactorily, or split it over two or more lessons.

Materials

Anything you need to get for the lesson. I have suggested paper sizes where appropriate.

Preparation

What you need to do before the lesson. I have tried to choose activities which involve you in as little preparation as possible.

In class

A step-by-step guide to what you do in class. No doubt you will adjust these suggestions to your own style and your children's needs.

Follow-up(s)

More things you might do once you have done the main activity.

Variations

Some alternative ideas which might be more appropriate to your class. Part of the ethos of this series is to encourage teachers to adapt and experiment. Find out what interests your children and help them to create stories about that.

1 Story warmers

The activities in this chapter provide general ideas for putting children in a 'story-making frame of mind'. They are not related to the specific story-making activities given in the rest of the book.

Some characteristics of a story-making frame of mind

It is difficult for anyone to invent a story suddenly without being in a story-making frame of mind. The activities in this chapter try to encourage the following:

- a willingness to 'have a go' and not worry about mistakes in the first draft
- a wish to explore and express personal experiences and ideas rather than reuse a set of clichés
- a delight in images and in language
- a wish to communicate clearly and simply
- a wish to communicate to others.

and, particularly in oral story-making:

- enjoyment of the sound and presence of words, voice, body, and meaning
- enjoyment and trust of the other people who are helping to make the story
- awareness and acceptance of the context of telling and listening.

To help you choose an appropriate warmer, they have been divided into five broad areas which help to develop the above:

- relaxation
- group dynamics
- trust
- mime and acting
- language.

However, they are not easy to classify as several overlap two or more of these areas. Some also help to develop other skills useful for story-making such as imagination (1.10, 1.13). Many of them can also be used as general warm-up activities, even if you are not intending to do a story-making activity afterwards.

Another good way to put children in a story-making frame of mind is to tell them stories, and to do some of the activities in the companion book, *Storytelling with Children*, which helps children respond actively to stories.

Relaxation

1.1 10 to 1

LEVEL   **All**

TIME   **10 minutes**

IN CLASS

1 Tell the children to relax and to close their eyes. Tell them that you will count very slowly from 10 to 1 and that you want them to concentrate on each number. Insist on total silence.

2 Count very slowly, giving the children time to feel the resonance and associations of each number. By the time you reach the number 1 the children will be relaxed and ready to begin the next activity.

1.2 Stretch

LEVEL   **All**

TIME   **10 minutes**

IN CLASS

1 All the children sit on the floor. They sit with their legs and knees close to their chests. They put their arms around their legs. They put their heads between their knees. They tighten the muscles of their legs, arms, back, neck, buttocks, feet, hands, and fingers—even the muscles in their faces!

2 They hold all their muscles tight for one minute and then slowly relax and loosen their muscles.

3 They should stand and slowly open out their arms, hands and fingers, and their legs. They should open their eyes and mouth as wide as possible.

Group dynamics

1.3 Class shout

LEVEL	**All**
TIME	**10 minutes**
IN CLASS	

1 All the class sit on the floor as close together as possible. One child acts as the leader and begins to make a low humming sound. Slowly other children begin to hum, and eventually everyone is humming, louder and louder.

2 As the humming gets louder the leader slowly begins to stand and others copy him or her. When everyone is on their feet (even if still crouching) everyone jumps in the air and shouts as loudly as possible.

3 Keep on doing this until it works smoothly and everyone is humming, rising, jumping, and shouting together. The class can choose a particular word or phrase to shout.

1.4 Class snake

LEVEL	**All**
TIME	**10 minutes**
IN CLASS	

1 All the children join hands in a long line. The first person (who must be strong, slow, considerate, and inventive!) leads the snake through itself: between bodies, between legs, over arms.

2 When the snake is in a complete knot, you or a child direct what each child must do to sort out the knot.

1.5 Copy me

LEVEL   **All**

TIME   **10 minutes**

IN CLASS
1 Arrange the children in circles of about eight. The first child in each circle makes a simple movement which all the other children copy, for example, rotating his or her head.
2 The next child copies the first action and then adds another, for example, rotating his or her head and then slapping his or her knee.

1.6 Pass the sound

LEVEL   **All**

TIME   **10 minutes**

IN CLASS
1 This can be done in groups or as a whole class. The children stand in circles of about eight children. The first child makes a short sound. The second child imitates the sound as closely as possible. The initiating child can correct any copying child. Each child in the circle copies each of the previous sounds before adding their own.
2 The children pass a word or short phrase round the circle.
3 The children pass round a word or a short phrase and try to imitate exactly the way it was spoken: intonation, stress, etc. You might suggest that the first child should try to express an emotion, for example, anger, happiness, surprise.

Trust

1.7 Puppet children

LEVEL   **All**

TIME   **10 minutes**

IN CLASS
1 Put the children into pairs. The 'A' children mould the 'B' children into any position they can. The position does not have to represent anything in particular. Play quiet music as the children are working.

After two minutes tell the 'A' children to stand back and admire their work.

2 The 'B' children should now try to walk about in the position they are in.

3 The 'B' children now model the 'A' children to be characters from stories.

1.8 Tick tock goes the clock

LEVEL   **All**

TIME   **10 minutes**

IN CLASS   In groups of three, the children stand in line. The first child turns to face the second. The second closes his or her eyes and then, keeping a stiff body, lets him- or herself fall backwards. The third child catches the middle child and gently pushes the middle child forward so that the first child must catch the middle child and push him or her back again.

1.9 Blind walk

LEVEL   **All**

TIME   **10 minutes**

IN CLASS   1 The children get into pairs. Child 'A' closes his or her eyes. Child 'B' leads his or her partner around the class, making sure that he/she doesn't bump into anything. After a few minutes Child 'B' should only use his/her fingertips.

2 Reverse roles.

3 (for Elementary level and above)

Reverse roles again. This time child 'B' should whisper descriptions of imaginary places they are both walking through.

Example

Child B: *We are walking through a wood. Be careful! It is dark and dangerous. I can hear an animal. Don't move. Now let's go. Be careful. Oh, here is a nice little animal. You can touch it.*

Mime and acting

1.10 Emotions

LEVEL   **All**

TIME   **10 minutes**

IN CLASS   **1** Write all the words for emotions and feelings the children know on the board.

Words might include: *happy, sad, angry, surprised, interested, worried.*

2 The children take it in turns to mime one of the words for the others to guess, first in pairs and then in groups.

1.11 Mime daily moments

LEVEL	**All**
TIME	**10 minutes**
IN CLASS	1 With the children's help write at least five moments from their everyday lives on the board.

Examples
waking up
eating breakfast
being late for the bus
being late for school

2 Ask a volunteer to mime one of the moments (without saying which one).

3 The other children call out what they think he or she was trying to express.

4 In groups, the children take it in turns to mime one of the moments. The other children guess which one is being mimed.

VARIATION   Other types of actions can also be mimed, for example emergency situations.

1.12 What's in the box?

LEVEL	**All**
TIME	**10 minutes**

IN CLASS

1 All the children sit around you in a circle. You mime:

picking up a box	*big/small/, heavy/light, confident/nervous*
opening it	*lock/string, difficult/easy, excited/happy/frightened*
finding something inside responding to it	*beautiful/revolting/frightening/amazing taking it out, cuddling it, stroking it/poking it with a finger, smiling/screaming*
closing the box	*regretfully/sadly/frightened slowly/suddenly/quickly*
putting it back	*regretfully/sadly/frightened slowly/suddenly/quickly*

2 When you have finished, ask the children to guess what you found in the box.

3 The children take it in turns to mime picking up another box and finding something else inside it.

1.13 Dramatic story moments

LEVEL	**All**
TIME	**10 minutes**
IN CLASS	1 With the children's help, write at least five dramatic moments from stories the children all know on the board. Each dramatic moment must involve two characters.

Examples

The wolf meets Little Red Riding Hood in the forest.
Robin Hood hides in a tree. The sheriff walks under the tree.
Beauty finds the Beast. He is lying in the garden.

2 Put the children into groups of six with three pairs of children in each. In pairs, they take it in turns to mime one of the dramatic moments. The other pairs guess which dramatic moment is being mimed.

1.14 Dramatic dialogues

LEVEL	**All**
TIME	**10 minutes**
IN CLASS	1 Write on the board four dramatic situations involving two people in each case.

Examples

walking across the desert
walking through town late at night
sitting and waiting for the bus to come
sitting and waiting for the giant to come home
hiding from the ice queen.

2 In pairs, the children choose one of the situations and plan and/or write a four- or six-line dialogue appropriate to it. They then act and rehearse their mini-situation.

3 All the pairs walk about the classroom, meeting other pairs and taking it in turns to act out their mini-situation. The audience pair must guess which situation the other pair has acted.

1.15 Creating characters

LEVEL	**All**
TIME	**10 minutes**

PREPARATION   On several pieces of paper, write adjectives which could describe story characters the children know. If necessary revise them first.

Examples
> *greedy, shy, stupid, friendly, kind, generous, angry, happy, intelligent, sad, funny.*

Make enough pieces of paper for each child to have one, even if it means that several children get the same adjective.

IN CLASS
1 Give out the pieces of paper. Each child thinks of a story character whom their adjective describes. They think of one sentence and one action that they think their character might say and do.
2 In groups, they take it in turns to say their sentence and perform their action.
3 Still in their groups, ask the children to form pairs in which the partners have different characters, and to work out a very short dialogue. They must decide where they are, the time of day, and the weather, and tell the rest of their group this before performing for them.

1.16 Robin Hood

LEVEL	**All**
TIME	**10 minutes**

IN CLASS
1 With the children's help, list up to eight stories they know on the board (in English or their mother tongue) and then list some of the characters.
2 The children stand in circles in groups of about eight.
3 Each child in turn says the name of a character from a story and then adopts a pose which is characteristic of that character.

1.17 Walk about

LEVEL	**All**
TIME	**10 minutes**

IN CLASS

1 The children walk about in a large, clear area of the classroom.

2 You stop them, perhaps with a bell or drum or clap of the hands. The children 'freeze' immediately and close their eyes. They then imagine a character or animal from a story.

3 They look at the character in their mind's eye and then open their eyes and walk about and behave as that character.

FOLLOW-UP

1 The children walk about, making contact with others and mumbling and grunting 'conversation'.

2 Now, if possible, they engage in conversation with another character.

Language

1.18 Fortunately–unfortunately

LEVEL	**All**
TIME	**10 minutes**

IN CLASS

1 All the children sit in a circle. You begin by describing a situation. The child next to you must then carry on the story, beginning with the word 'fortunately'. The next child continues the story with 'unfortunately'. Each child must listen to what the previous child has said in order to make the relevant contrast.

Example

You:	*This story is about a boy and his mother and father. The boy's name is Tom. Tom is not happy. He wants a pet.*
Child A:	*Fortunately, his mother gives him a pet.*
Child B:	*Unfortunately, the pet is a crocodile.*
Child C:	*Fortunately, it is a nice crocodile.*
Child D:	*Unfortunately, it eats children.*

VARIATION

This is a good opportunity to practise intonation:

fortunately   ↗   (rise to show positive aspect)
unfortunately   ↘   (fall to show negative aspect)

If the rise and fall are exaggerated it can become very funny.

1.19 Auditions

LEVEL   **All**

TIME   **10 minutes**

PREPARATION   Write on the board a single sentence which is (or could be) the beginning of a story.

Example

'You can come with us or you can stay here!' he said.

IN CLASS   1 The children sit in circles of about six. They take it in turns to read the sentence you have given them. They should each try to read it in several different ways. The other children must recommend to them the best way.

2 The groups each choose their favourite way of saying the sentence. The chosen child reads the sentence to the whole class in their special way.

2 The craft of story-making

We must not let children think there is only one way to make a story. Some authors research a topic for a year before beginning to form the story in their mind. Other authors might have a general feel of what they want to do and perhaps an idea of a person and a place, and then just begin! Twenty more authors will have twenty different ways of going about their story-making.

The suggestions in this section on the craft of story-making are not meant to be techniques which *must* be followed. Let the children try them out and experience them and see if they are useful to them.

Some characteristics of good story-making

This chapter is divided into five sections on different aspects of story-making.

Particularizing

It is easier to generalize about experiences than it is to particularize, but it is the particular detail in description or dialogue which makes a story come alive for other people.

Bubbling

It is easy to adopt the first thing which comes into your head, but sometimes that is a bit ordinary and general. Take time to wander in your mind until you find that special idea.

Clustering

Take time to find links between your bits and pieces of ideas—there might be a very special connection to find.

Desires and difficulties

Look for links between the pieces of information which come to you in your wandering search for the seeds of stories. Desires and difficulties are central to a story's plot. Most stories centre around the idea that somebody wants something but there is a difficulty.

Planning and sequencing

Now you must sequence the events of your story for your readers and listeners. How are you going to begin and how will you unfold your tale? You must engage the reader or listener, be clear, and hold their interest in the way you describe the people and places, introduce desires and difficulties, and how you get the characters to struggle to overcome the difficulties. Finally, you need to wrap up the story with some kind of solution, happy or unhappy.

Particularizing

If we want to be able to see a picture in our mind's eye, the description must not be too general. Creating a picture in our imagination is often possible even with the limited language of a child in their first year of English. For example:

> *The man has a dog.*
> *The little man has a very big dog.*
> *The thin, little man has a very big, grey dog.*

What can the author and/or the people in the story see, hear, feel, smell, and taste which is important to them? What do the people say, think, and feel?

Show the children how to make word webs as a way of looking for details and the language needed. Here are two examples at different proficiency levels:

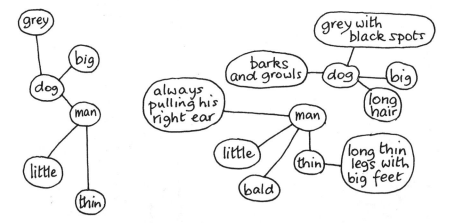

Show the children how they can visualize the stories they hear and use the same technique to improve their own. For example, as you tell the class a story, suddenly stop and ask them to tell you what they see (it is best to ask the children to close their eyes and to rest their heads on their arms). What does the cottage in the forest look like? Is it big or small? How many windows has it got? What colour are the walls? What colour is the door? Are there any curtains? Is it old or new? All these details can be given with the simplest of words.

2.1 Particularizing people

In this activity the children make wall-size profile portraits of other children in the class.

LEVEL	**Beginners (can be adapted for elementary and above)**
LANGUAGE	**Fluency in the four skills with an emphasis on writing**
TIME	**30–40 minutes**
MATERIALS	A large piece of white paper for each student. A larger piece for the demonstration poster.
PREPARATION	Draw a large, empty line silhouette of a figure approximating to yourself on the poster.

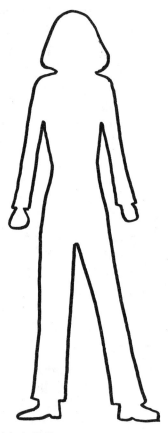

IN CLASS

1 Display the large poster. Explain that the class will do studies of everyone in the class, including you. You will show them how to do their study by taking yourself as an example.

2 Ask one or two of the more able artists in the class to sketch details onto the line silhouette you have prepared. Encourage them to emphasize your features slightly! As they draw, ask the class to call out a descriptive phrase or sentence, for example:

You've got a big nose. You've got kind eyes.

Write these observations near the feature referred to.

3 Write on the board some phrases the children know for describing people's appearance, behaviour, personality, likes/dislikes, hopes, possessions, hobbies, abilities, habits, desires and difficulties, etc.

He likes ...
She doesn't like ...
He's got ...
She wants ...
He can ...
She is ...

4 Ask the class to call out any other observations they feel are accurate. Tell them that they can ask you questions about yourself, ranging from, for example, *Have you got a pet?* to (with higher-proficiency students) *What makes you frightened/angry?* etc.

Write their statements on the poster: *She's got an old cat. He's frightened of dogs.*

5 All the children write their names on small pieces of paper. Redistribute the lists at random. The children then each make a portrait study of the child whose name they have been given. The drawing and the written observations should be truthful and focus on the individual quality of the person.

2.2 Particularizing places

This activity helps children to appreciate the character of the place they are in. Even the most ordinary place has character!

LEVEL

Elementary and above

LANGUAGE

Fluency in the four skills with an emphasis on writing

TIME

30–40 minutes

IN CLASS

1 Tell the class to rest their heads on their arms, to close their eyes, and then to listen to all the sounds inside and outside the classroom. After a few minutes ask the children to open their eyes and to quietly write down everything they heard. You can suggest to the children that they divide their paper into two parts.

They might write:

Inside	*Outside*
Mathew (breathing)	birds were singing
(someone) laughing	cars (going along the road)
(someone dropped) a pencil	a woman (walking in the corridor) (people) talking

2 Ask the children to work in groups of four and to compare notes. They should add some of the things the others heard, if they heard them too but did not note them down. This is also a time to ask you for help with the language.

3 Have a general class sharing of sounds they heard. Ask if they would hear different sounds at different times of the day. Agree with the class on three other times in the day and write them down on the board, for example,

midday   5.00 p.m.   midnight

The class imagine the sounds they might hear then. If they imagine voices they should write down what they think the people are saying.

FOLLOW-UP 1

The children have now used their ears to study their classroom. Do a similar study with each of the five senses.

FOLLOW-UP 2

The children can take the observations they have made and list them in poem-like form.

VARIATION

Ask the children to call out as many different words and phrases describing their classroom as they can, making use of all their senses. Encourage the children to add adjectives and/or prepositions to nouns to make each one special in some way.

2.3 Particularizing objects

LEVEL

Elementary and above

LANGUAGE

Speaking, describing objects

TIME

30 minutes

IN CLASS

1 Describe an object which you know the children are familiar with. It must be an individual object, for example, your car— not just any car of the same make.

The children must try to identify what you are describing and then discuss with you what helped them to understand which individual object it was.

2 Ask the children to describe an object which they believe the other children know well by answering questions such as these:

How heavy is it?   *How does it feel?*
How big is it?   *How does it work?*
What shape is it?   *Whose is it?*
What colour is it?   *How rare or valuable is it?*
What is it made of?

3 The children now describe their object to at least three other children and see how many of them can name what they have described.

VARIATION

Bring in a few objects which are important to you in some way. Talk about them and point out their character: scratches, cracks, etc. Tell the children what you associate with the objects. Encourage the children to do the same.

The children can then make a drawing of one of these objects, or one which is important to them, and write words and phrases around the drawing.

2.4 Particularizing situations

LEVEL   **Elementary and above**

LANGUAGE   **Fluency in all the skills with an emphasis on speaking**

TIME   **30–40 minutes**

1 Mime a short story for the whole class. Here is an example:

> An old man is walking along. It's snowing and he's cold. He sees a house. He knocks on the door. He waits for a moment then he knocks again. He opens the door and goes into the house. It's warm! There are no people in the house. He opens the door of a room. It's very warm in the room and there's a table. On the table there is some food. He eats some of the food and then he sits in the armchair and sleeps.
>
> In the morning he wakes up. He stands up. He is happy. He jumps! He dances! He sings and then he looks in a mirror. He is not the same man!

2 Mime the whole story once and then ask the children to say what they think you were doing. The children can just call out single words if they wish. If the children are correct you can write their words on the board. Note: the end of the story is difficult for children to interpret: tell them in the mother tongue.

3 Mime the story again and stop after each action. Ask the children to say what you were doing. Write their words or phrases on the board if they are correct.

4 Now tell the story, making use of all the words supplied by the children. Alternatively, ask the class to do this together.

5 Ask the children to tell you about any other things they can imagine in the story:

What is the man wearing? Hat? Coat? Colour? New or old?
How is he walking? (slowly/quickly)
How does he feel? (tired/hungry)
What can he see/hear/feel/smell/taste?
What does he think and feel?
Does he speak? What does he say?

Bubbling and clustering

This approach to writing stories is for authors who wander and wonder in their minds as they see, hear, feel, smell, and touch their memories and associations. All you can do is to gently help launch the children launch themselves inwards, into their own minds. Nuzzle them along with suggestions, and above all make them feel that their apparently undirected wanderings are worthwhile.

If the technique of bubbling and clustering is new to the children, they may need time to get used to it. That might apply to you as well.

Once the children are used to bubbling and clustering, they will bubble and cluster without your help. However, it is important to note that some people really do not find this 'brainstorming' approach useful. They like to go straight into their story.

2.5 Birthday bubbles

LEVEL	**Elementary and above**
LANGUAGE	**Fluency in all four skills leading to accuracy in the final writing**
TIME	**30–40 minutes**

IN CLASS

1 Write a word such as *birthday* (or name day or other important day in your children's year) on the board.

2 Ask the children to call out anything they can think of related to their own experience of birthdays (not just the general idea of birthdays).

When children call out words or phrases, ask them where you should write them. If they are connected to any of the others put them together (clustering). Otherwise put them in separate bubbles.

Encourage the children to think of:

– information through all their five senses
– things they remember people said, felt, or thought.

They should be as particular as possible: for example, not just 'cake' but 'big cake' or 'very big chocolate cake'.

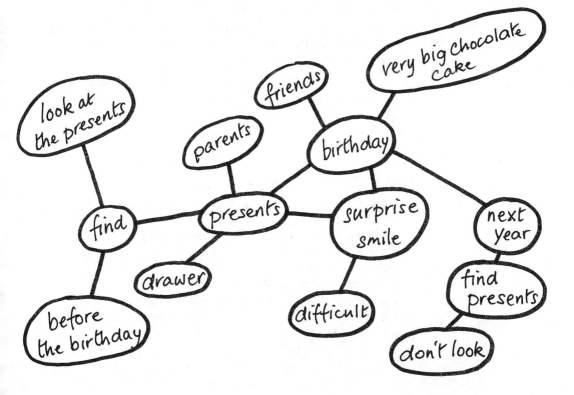

3 Encourage and highlight desires and problems the children associate with the topic (see page 33). These will be the seeds of the story—the rest of the information will just help the children to describe the situation.

Encourage the children to use their imaginations, not just their own experiences. You can supply new words if necessary. Do not insist on full sentences.

Example

mother   presents in a drawer   look   open presents   smile

This could become a story about a boy or girl whose mother hides his or her presents before their birthday. He or she finds them and opens them to have a look and puts them back again. The mother knows but does not tell the child. The child then finds it very difficult at the birthday party. Next year he or she finds the presents before the birthday again, but does not look at them and closes the drawer.

4 Ask the children if they want to add any more bubbles of ideas.

5 Ask them for various ways of starting and then sequencing ideas based on the bubbles. Give each bubble a number as they decide where it should be in the sequence.

6 Draft a first paragraph on the board with the children's help.

FOLLOW-UP

1 The children bubble down their ideas, cluster them, and begin to look for connections that could make a story.

2 The children show their bubbling and clustering to a friend and discuss it. In this way the children may see other ideas, and their story might emerge through conversation.

3 Once the storyline has begun to emerge the children might want to enrich some of the detail through 'particularization'.

4 They plan the sequence of ideas in the story by numbering the bubbles.

5 The children write their first draft.

VARIATIONS

Instead of starting from a set topic, use one of these ideas:

– display a large picture which you think will be evocative for the children
– display a lot of little pictures, for example, postcards, and ask the children to choose one
– play some music
– show the children an object
– ask the children to think of a place or a person
– ask the children to draw a picture of something which is important to them.

Desires and difficulties in stories

In Eric Hill's classic children's book *Where's Spot?*, Spot's mother wants him to come and have his dinner (desire) but she cannot find him (difficulty). When she finds him the story is over. However, in some stories the desires and difficulties are not so apparent. In *The Very Hungry Caterpillar* by Eric Carle, the desire is obvious—the caterpillar wants to eat and eat. The difficulty is not so apparent, and we read to find out what the difficulty is going to be. In the end there is no real difficulty, just the drama of change from caterpillar to chrysalis to butterfly.

We should not haunt children with the restrictive maxim that there must be desires and difficulties in every story. However, we can give the children experiences of story-making (and appreciation of existing stories) which help them to build up a sense of the need for some sort of dramatic tension caused by the conflict between desire and difficulty, or wondering what is going to happen next.

Look for every opportunity to talk about the importance of desires, difficulties, and dramatic tension in stories, and how the story is a struggle to achieve the desire(s). Once the problems are settled, one way or another, the story is finished.

Accept that a problem may not be as obvious as falling in a deep hole or being threatened by a wolf. A problem may be simply that you want to go to sleep and somebody stops you from doing so.

Examine stories the children know and talk about the desires and difficulties in them (usually there are several major desires and many minor desires in every story).

2.6 Someone in a hole

This activity aims to develop in the children an increased awareness of the importance of 'desires' and 'difficulties' in stories.

LEVEL	**Elementary and above**
LANGUAGE	**Questions, fluency in all four skills**
TIME	**Steps 1 to 3: 30 minutes, plus 30 minutes for steps 4 and 5.**
MATERIALS	Two pieces of white paper for each child (about 30 cm x 40 cm). Thin card for the class book (about 40 cm x 60 cm can make two books).

IN CLASS

1 Draw this picture on the board. Draw the hole first of all. Ask the children what you are drawing. Make sure they know the word *hole*. Also teach the word *deep*. Draw the person (at this point we do not know if it is a man or woman—get the children to decide).

2 Ask questions:

Is it a man, a woman, a boy, or a girl?
How old is he/she?
What is his/her name? Do we know?
What is he/she doing?
How does he/she feel? Is he/she happy, unhappy, angry, frightened?
Why is he/she in the hole?
Did he/she fall in the hole?
Did somebody put him/her into the hole?

3 Pairs of children work together to write the story so far and then to write the end of the story—how the person got out. Let each pair ask for up to three new words. Put all new words (with their translations, if necessary) on the board so that any children can use them.

4 Once their draft has been revised and approved by you, each child is responsible for writing the story neatly and for doing either the first illustration of the person in the hole or the

second one of how the person got out. The simple stick figure which you drew on the board should be 'fleshed out' by the children into the character which they imagine.

5 Use one of the techniques for making books given in Chapter 8 to make a class book called *The Hole*.

COMMENTS

Discuss the story with the children at every reasonable opportunity, to make them see that the most important thing is what the person in the hole wants and what his or her difficulty is in achieving this—the struggle to achieve the desire is the story. The children may, of course, have written a story in which the hole itself is not the problem. The person may have jumped into the hole because a monster was chasing him or her—in which case the problem is the monster!

VARIATION 1

1 Draw a picture of a face on a large piece of paper on the wall or board. Ask the children to tell you how to draw the face.

2 Get the children to invent a name and an age for their character.

3 Now say *Want! Want! Want! That is what his mother always said!*

Draw three bubbles around his or her head: *wants to do, wants to have, wants to be.*

4 Ask the children to suggest what the character wants to do, have, or be. Write their ideas in the bubbles.

5 Now ask the children why he can't do, have, or be those things. Write their suggestions in red.

6 Divide all the characters' wants among the children so that they can write up each one as a story. Tell them he can either get what he wants or not get it but there must be a conclusion. Tell them they have only got one side of paper for their story because you want to make a book of all the stories. They must invent the title.

VARIATION 2

Instead of asking the children to write the desires and difficulties, give them a list and ask them to match one 'want' with one difficulty. There is, of course, no right or wrong matching.

Wants to do	Wants to be	Wants to have	Difficulty
climb high mountains	a famous singer	a fast car	no money
find his brother	funny	a goldfish	it's snowing
sleep	thin	CD player	a witch

2.7 Comparing problem picture stories

This activity is intended to help the children develop their awareness of the drama of 'desire and difficulty' in stories.

LEVEL

Elementary and above

LANGUAGE

Questions, simple past tense and past continuous

TIME

30–40 minutes

PREPARATION

1 Make sure the children have already done activity 2.6, 'Someone in a hole'.

2 Photocopy the set of four problem pictures. Cut them into four separate pictures. Make sure there are enough pictures so that each pair of children will get one picture.

N CLASS

1 Remind the children of the stories they wrote called *The Hole*. Through questions focus the children's minds on the importance of desires, difficulties, and dramatic tension in their stories, and how the story is a struggle to achieve the desire(s). For example:

What does this person want? Why?
What can he/she do?

2 Arrange the children in pairs. Give each pair a problem picture. Remind them of the questions they should ask themselves (you might like to write them on the board):

Is it a man, a woman, a boy, or a girl?
How old is he/she?
What is his/her name? Do we know?
How does he/she feel? Happy? Unhappy? Angry? Frightened?
Where is he/she?
What is he/she doing?
Why are they doing that?

3 The children should now work out what has happened and what is going to happen next. They should decide what the person or people want and what the difficulties are, where they are, and how they struggle to overcome them. They should then create their story and adapt their problem picture into a new illustration appropriate to their story.

4 The children now find another pair of children with the same picture. They exchange stories and listen to or read what the other pair have made up. If the children have any questions, they should talk to the pair who invented the story.

2.8 Making problem pictures

LEVEL	**Pre-intermediate**
LANGUAGE	**Simple past tense and past continuous, writing**
TIME	**30–40 minutes**
PREPARATION	Make sure the children have done 2.6, 'Someone in a hole', and/or 2.7, 'Comparing problem picture stories'. The children must be familiar with the idea of the centrality of desires and difficulties in stories.
IN CLASS	1 Remind the children of the pictures they used in their previous activity and of the importance of having a difficulty in their story (or a feeling that there might be a difficulty at any time!). Remind them that difficulties do not have to be huge like being in a deep hole! It might be a difficulty that you are tired but mustn't go to sleep because it is still lesson time!

2 In pairs, the children draw their own problem picture in which one or more people clearly have a desire and a difficulty.

If some children cannot think of what to draw ask them to think of a boy or girl of their age and of a problem they might have. Then they should draw a picture which suggests that problem. For example, being lonely, being bullied, being frightened, wanting something they cannot have, wanting to do something which is not allowed, and so on.

3 Tell the children to write a short story about their picture in which the problem is in some way resolved—either happily or

unhappily. Tell them they will have exactly ten minutes and will have to stop then even if they have not finished.

4 They should now exchange their picture with another pair and write a story about the other pair's picture in exactly 10 minutes.

5 They compare stories written about the same picture.

6 If the stories have not been completed they can now be written to their final conclusion.

VARIATION

Show how the story can be written with limited English. It can be in note form or just a couple of lines long. For example, if the picture shows a child stuck in a tree, the child could write:

She can't get down.
She shouts.
She falls down.

In Step 6 they could write: *She is hurt. She is in hospital. Her friends bring chocolate.*

FOLLOW-UP

1 Discuss with the children all the sorts of desires, difficulties, and struggles to overcome the problems they invented for their stories and how they were 'answered' for better or for worse by the end of the story.

2 Examine stories or television series the children know and ask them to tell you what sort of problems the characters have in those stories.

COMMENTS

This activity is intended to help develop the children's awareness of the central importance of desires, difficulties, and struggles to overcome problems in stories.

Planning stories

It should be emphasized, once more, that techniques such as those given here are not the way for children to create their stories. Each technique should be seen as a way of extending the child's experience and for him or her to develop and make use of later if it seems natural to do so.

Introduce the idea of structuring stories by looking at stories the children know already. Let their reflection on the structure of the story be accompanied by action: no theoretical analysis! Many of the activities in *Storytelling with Children* are useful for this.

2.9 A three-part story

LEVEL

Elementary and above

LANGUAGE

Fluency in listening and speaking

TIME

30–40 minutes

MATERIALS

A clothes line or strong string. About ten clothes pegs.

PREPARATION

1 If you can, get hold of a copy of *Where's Spot?* If not, spend two minutes jotting down the sort of places where a puppy might be hiding (see Comments, below) and make sure you can tell the story.

2 Fasten the clothes line from one side of the room to the other, near the front.

IN CLASS

1 Tell the story.

2 Ask the children to retell the story. You can help them by eliciting information.

3 Put the children into pairs and ask each pair to make a large picture of a scene from the story (one scene each).

4 Ask the children to retell the story and one child from each pair to stand in a line, in the correct sequence, holding their pictures.

5 Tie the clothes line across the room. Clip the pictures onto the line. Retell the story with the children. Introduce the phrases and words: *At the beginning … and then … in the end.* Emphasize these stages, but be careful not to suggest that all stories are like that!

VARIATION

You can of course use other stories, depending on the children's age and level of English.

FOLLOW-UP

With older children, discuss what would happen if the order of events were changed. Try it on the clothes line. Discuss the advantages and disadvantages of a different sequence.

COMMENTS

1 This activity is based on Eric Hill's classic children's book about a mother dog and her puppy, *Where's Spot?* The story can be divided into three parts:

1 Spot's mother wants Spot to eat his dinner but she doesn't know where he is (situation, protagonists, problem).

2 She looks for him under the stairs, in the clock, under the bed, and in several other places. In each place there is another animal (action, struggle, surprise).

3 She finds Spot (conclusion/resolution).

2 See 5.2, 'Clothes line story', for more ways of using a clothes line.

2.10 Three-part flowchart story

LEVEL

Elementary and above

LANGUAGE

Fluency in all four skills

TIME

30 minutes for Steps 1 to 3, plus 30 minutes for Step 4

PREPARATION

Before introducing the flowchart it is better for the children to have experienced the clothes line and its demonstration of story planning (see 2.9).

IN CLASS

1 Draw and write this flowchart on the board:

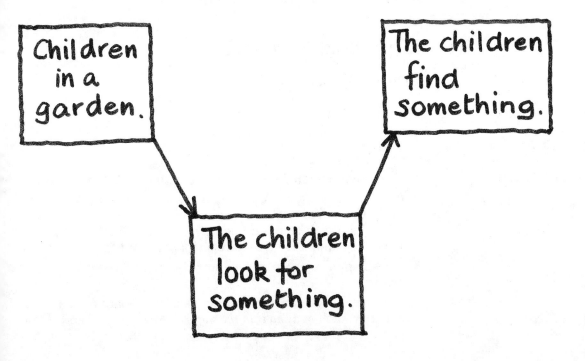

2 Ask the children as many questions as you can think of about the sentences in these three boxes. For example:
How many children are there?
Who are they? How old are they?
Are they friends?
Is it a big garden or a little garden?
Where are they looking?
What do they find?
Is it easy or difficult?

3 Tell the story, using the children's ideas and their language as much as possible. Continually refer to the flowchart, pointing to the box you are 'in'. Demonstrate in this way that the flowchart is a planning device. It is not necessary, however, to say this explicitly.

4 As the class speculate orally together on what might happen in one of the flowcharts you can list useful words and phrases on the board.

5 Give each child three pieces of paper. Ask the children to write a story guided by the flowchart and the various words and phrases you have noted down. Tell them to use the three sheets of paper, one for the beginning, middle, and end of the story, each one related to one of the flowchart boxes. This will help remind the children to stick to the three-part structure.

FOLLOW-UP

Tell them that a three-part story is only one way of making a story. Even 'Little Red Riding Hood' is more complicated than that. Analyse other stories (such as 'Little Red Riding Hood') into a flowchart of boxes (see 2.11).

2.11 Eight-box flowchart

LEVEL

Elementary and above

LANGUAGE

Fluency in all skills

TIME

30 minutes

IN CLASS

1 Draw eight rectangles on the board with spaces between them.

2 Ask volunteers to come up and draw something, each drawing in a different rectangle. Only give them 30 seconds each (to show that the drawings do not need to be perfect). At this stage they do not need to have a story in mind.

3 Now help the class to make a story based on the eight pictures.

If necessary you can write questions on the board to guide the children, such as *Who is in the story? Where are they?* and so on.

Let them take the questions and pictures in any sequence they wish. Do they want to start with a person? Do they want to introduce the place immediately? The answers will depend partly on the pictures and partly on their imagination. Once they have decided, draw arrows connecting the boxes.

Example

VARIATION 1

1 Draw eight boxes on the board. Ask volunteers to draw pictures, each drawing in a different rectangle. The pictures do not have to be related.

2 In threes, the children invent a story which connects all the pictures.

3 Each group, in turn, stands by the board and tells the story, pointing at the pictures as they do so.

4 Ask the artists to say what they had in mind (if anything).

VARIATION 2

The children draw their pictures on pieces of paper which are then stuck to the board. If you use this method make sure the children use big black markers so that their drawings can be seen.

VARIATION 3

1 Prepare seven envelopes of magazine photos and write on each envelope one of the following:

People	Places	Objects	Desires	Difficulties	Action	End

2 Tell the children to work in pairs or groups and to choose two pictures from each envelope (but one from 'end'), decide on a sequence, and lay them out on their table.

3 They then take it in turns to visit another group and first of all to guess the other group's story from their sequence and then to listen to the story they have created.

Stories from experience

It is important for children to feel that they can make stories out of their own experience, not just rely on the stories they receive from other people. It is also important for children to feel that they can explore their experience and express their feelings about it through the foreign or second language—even if their command of it is much more limited than their first language.

A story-making climate

The children must feel that you care about what they are trying to say, not just how they are saying it. They must feel that you enjoy and value their stories.

Releasers

We have to provide ways of helping the children to find a door into their memories and feelings. One principle is to choose topics which are relatively narrow. For example, *What makes me happy* is too vague. *A happy moment this morning* is more limiting and therefore easier to do.

Here are some story title releasers used successfully by teachers:

A toy of mine
Some of my earliest memories
Cruel things done to animals
Accidents at school
A particular time when I was ill
Scars on my body and what happened
My first school day
My worst teacher
An important person in my life
One place where many things have happened

A title on its own is rarely enough to stimulate children. You must encourage discussion of the topic with volunteers, including yourself, exchanging memories, however briefly. In this way the mind of each child begins to stir.

Sometimes it is helpful for the children to make a drawing or a map representing a place or an incident. By concentrating on making the map, the children find themselves taken into their past. They then can explain what happened there, and through this explanation the story is born.

Sometimes it is helpful to ask the children to bring an object (or objects) or a photograph (or photographs) from home. Holding the picture or object helps to release the child.

You might ask the children to place their objects in a special order on their tables. Ask them to walk around the class and look at the arrangements of other children and then ask them to bubble (see pages 30–31). Sometimes you might ask the child to mime what happened so that the other children can guess.

A carefully selective description of one's experience can sometimes lead to a story. Another way of using one's own experience as a basis for story-making is to say, 'What if ...' and to combine two (or more) experiences which were not combined in your experience. Two bits of truth combine into a new, imaginative truth.

2.12 What if ...

LEVEL Elementary and above

LANGUAGE Fluency in listening and speaking

TIME 20–30 minutes

IN CLASS 1 Suggest that you and the class make a story. Help the children to list on the board five places and five animals they know well.

Example

kitchen	dog
supermarket	mouse
cupboard	bird
swimming pool	crocodile
classroom	monkey

2 Choose two of the words, for example, crocodile and supermarket. What if there is a crocodile in the supermarket? Write the two words on the board and then cluster around them all the words and phrases which occur to the children related to the place and the animal.

3 Now help the children move into sequencing events to make the story. Look for desires and difficulties (see page 33)—this should not be too difficult with a crocodile in a supermarket. Ask helpful questions (but not questions which imply that you have already thought of the story!). If you feel it would be helpful, you can draw the sequence as a flowchart on the board.

4 Ask the children to work in pairs or threes, and to bubble and sequence ideas related to another animal and place pairings and then to create their own story.

VARIATION

Other 'What if' combinations might include: people and accidents; objects, places, and people; extraordinary abilities and people; extraordinary objects and people.

3 Retelling

In the activities in this chapter the children retell a story they have heard or read. They retell it exactly or with changes.

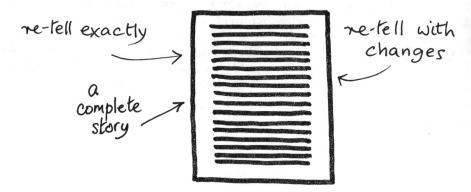

Why retelling?

Retelling stories is as old as time; we all do it every day. For language teaching it is rich in many ways:

– it is repetition with a purpose
– it demands a sustained oral or written flow of coherent language
– it allows for personal adaptation and response to audience and context
– it is a natural activity for even very young children (obviously they do it in their own way!)
– it is easy for the teacher to organize
– it gives children confidence in their ability to tell stories
– it acts as a bridge between responding to stories and creating their own.

Retelling with limited language

It is possible to retell most stories with the most limited range of language; giving children plenty of opportunity to do so will develop their fluency (for examples, see page 3). Of course, the children are going to make mistakes or may not even find the words they need. Retelling, like all story-making, is a challenge to do what you can with what you have got. You can help by:

– keeping to the general principle of more oral than written retelling

- preceding written retelling with oral retelling
- making sure that key words and phrases are available to the children
- accepting a list of words and phrases in the correct sequence rather than full sentences if necessary
- being a sympathetic audience more interested in the story than in inaccuracies of language while the story is being told (you can give grammatically focused activities at another time).

Retelling more or less exactly

Stories, jokes, songs, poems, and plays are retold and sung many times. If children like a story, they can see a reason for learning to retell it—they can share it with others and learn to savour it more for themselves. It also boosts their confidence to see that they can really tell a story in English. I remember a ten-year-old Danish girl who listened to me tell a story and then managed to tell it to her mother in English. At the end she was stunned with what she had achieved. She said, 'I talked for ten minutes and I told a story in English!'

Even if we can remember the words exactly, it can still be difficult to retell a story exactly—think of the many ways in which producers can present Shakespeare's plays! So, even if children retell a story more or less as they heard it, there is still opportunity for creativity. It is the way a story is retold which provides the opportunity for personal expression. This is particularly apparent when a story is retold in written form—children can make a book or a poster and spend time designing titles and illustrations which express their feelings about the story.

Prompting retelling with questions

The established way of getting the children to retell a story is to do so as a class. You ask the children:

Can you remember the story?
Who is in the story?
How does the story begin?

You can make use of all the question types: *who, where, when, what, why,* etc.

Your questions remind the children of the storyline and help them to fill it out with detail.

Alternatively, higher-proficiency children can invent ten questions with you which will lead to answers which retell the story.

A bare bones retelling

You might retell the story yourself in its barest form and then ask the children to add whatever they can remember. The children can ask you questions to get more detail. These questions can expand the story beyond the original, for example, *How old is she? What colour is her hair?*

Prompting with pictures, key phrases, mime, etc.

You can use any of the following to prompt the children's memory:

- *a sequence of pictures* which prompt their memory or which they have to arrange into the right order. The pictures can be copied from a book, drawn by you as sketches on the board, or drawn by the children.
- *a sequence of key phrases*: these can be on long strips of card or paper. The children can hold them and stand in sequence to tell the story. Alternatively, the strips can be arranged on the board in the correct sequence.
- *a sequence of key words*: this is more demanding on the children than giving full sentences. You can either give the class the key words, or elicit them through discussion.
- *mime*: you might mime the story and encourage the children with gestures to interpret your mime correctly.
- *figurines, puppets*: you or the children operate figurines or puppets and give some verbal clues if necessary.

With some classes you may have to do most of the retelling yourself, asking the children to supply only limited bits of information. For example, you might bend down and pretend to pick flowers, saying, *And Little Red Riding Hood picks ...?*

In her rich book in this series, *Young Learners*, Sarah Phillips suggests that you sketch the story picture-by-picture on the board and refuse to speak. Before you begin you can claim you have a very sore throat! The children have to supply the story, prompted by the pictures you draw.

Favourite bits only

Instead of asking for the whole story you can ask the children to think of their favourite part of the story and just retell that. If possible cover the whole story in this way and get the children to sequence their contributions in order to tell the complete story. You can ask the children to draw a picture of one part of a story they like and write just a sentence or two. If your children are more proficient you can ask them to retell their bits in greater detail.

Retelling with changes

Here are some reasons why children might make changes to a story.

Personal reasons

Without being asked to do so, most people will actually select, heighten, omit, and add details to a story to make it their own. You might find that it helps the children if you discuss the story with them before they retell it. *Do you like the story? Which is the best bit of the story? What do you think of Little Red Riding Hood? Is she sensible or stupid? Do you like the ending?*

You can ask each child to think of their favourite bit of the story and then use that to start their personal retelling (see above). Alternatively, if the children are writing they might only write the first paragraph and all these first paragraphs can be displayed. This allows intensity of experience and writing without having to sustain it for a whole story.

A different medium

To retell a story you have heard or read in one medium into another, you must make creative changes to it. You can ask the children to:
- write the story and illustrate it in book form (see Chapter 8)
- prepare/write a dramatic version for audio or video recording
- prepare/write a dramatic version for a puppet, mask, or shadow play.

You can add restrictions which will make the children think hard:
- for a book, you might stipulate that it must be eight pages long including the cover, and it must not have more than 250 words in total
- for a tape, you might say that a group's performance must last exactly three minutes and consist of three one-minute episodes.

Points of view

You can ask the children to tell the story from the point of view of one of the protagonists or antagonists, for example, the wolf in 'Little Red Riding Hood': 'I was very hungry. I saw a girl and I wanted to eat her'.

A child could pretend to be an object in the story and retell the story from its point of view: 'I am a tree in a forest. There are a lot of flowers in the forest. One day a wolf came ...'

Children could wear a mask, wig, make-up, or character clothes and be interviewed as if he or she were one of the characters or objects in the story (perhaps by you so that you can be as helpful as possible).

Each child could imagine he or she is a person, animal, or object in the story and then walk about introducing him or herself. Then, in pairs or groups, the children can tell their versions of the story and even argue about it.

A child in role as a person, animal, or object can be interviewed by the class and, in this way, retell the story (see 'Forest News' in *Storytelling with Children*, page 186).

If the points of view of all the characters and inanimate objects are written up, they can be collected together and made into a book.

Different settings

The children can change the geographical or historical setting of the story. For example, 'Little Red Riding Hood' could take place in a city.

Ask the children to retell the story based on people and places they know well. They might even use the names and characters of people in the class and the school neighbourhood.

Changing ideas, feelings, and values

The children can take a serious story and make it as silly as they like. Here is an example, by a Hungarian student: 'Little Red Riding Hood rode her red motorbike. She went to her grandmother. She carried hamburgers in her basket ...'

The children can retell the story with everything the opposite way round, for example, Little Red Riding Hood becomes Big Black Riding Boots!

The children can change:
- a hero into a heroine
- foolish behaviour into brave behaviour
- the genre: a legend into a newspaper report
- the ending.

Expanding or reducing the story

The children can change the quantity of information by:
- adding an episode before, during, or after the story
- adding an extra person (which could be the child him or herself!)
- cutting out a scene they think is silly
- combining two characters into one.

Combining two stories

The children create a new story by combining elements of two different stories, for example, 'Little Red Riding Hood and the three bears'.

A special listener or reader

Children can be motivated to modify a story for a special audience. For example, children of 13 or 14 who have studied English for a few years can visit a class of younger children and tell them stories. They must take into account the children's younger age and limited knowledge of English.

Rumour research

Stories are changed in retelling. The traditional 'Chinese whispers' game is an example of this.

Improving the story

The children can try improving the story by:
- changing the order of situations in it
- adding more detail about the people, the place, or the action
- enriching the language.

Parallel stories

A story can act as a model for a new story. For example, tell a creation myth to the children and ask them to invent a new one, using the one you have given as a guide. Most cultures offer a variety of stories which explain the origin of the world, particular places, animals, or happenings.

Pattern books

Children can make pattern books based on an existing book which makes use of the basic sentence pattern(s) used in it. This is a very easy and effective way of helping the children to create a story with the most limited amount of language. Typical patterns might include:

Where's X? Is he under the table? No, he isn't.
What do you want? I want X.
Let's X.
First of all she X, then she Y, then she Z.

(For making books see Chapter 8.)

Organizing oral retelling

Retelling with the whole class has been described above.

Pairs with the same stories

Tell two stories to the whole class and then put the children into pairs. Ask each child to try to retell one of the stories to their partner. The listening partner must help if he or she can.

Pairs with different stories

Divide the class into two groups. Tell one group a story outside the classroom. Leave a tape recorder to play a story you have previously recorded to the other group.

Make pairs with one child from each group. Each child takes it in turns to retell the story they heard.

Triads with different parts

Divide the class into three equal groups. Give each group a different part of the story to learn. Then make groups of three children, one from each large group. They tell each other their part of the story.

It is easiest to give the parts of the story to the children in the written form.

Two classes and two stories

If you have two classes of similar proficiency level, tell each class a different story. Make sure every child is capable of retelling their class's story. Bring the two classes together and make pairs with one child from each class. They take it in turns to tell their story.

3.1 Changing words

LEVEL	**Pre-intermediate**
LANGUAGE	**Simple past tense; intensive reading**
TIME	**20–30 minutes**
PREPARATION	1 Find a text in which some of the key words can be substituted by others your children know. You might underline those words which you feel the children can change which would not cause significant grammatical or syntactical change.

2 Write the text on the board before the lesson.

Example

> I found a small dragon in the garden. I think it came from the
> middle of a dark forest. It was wet and green and there were
> leaves on its back. I gave it many things: grass, leaves, flowers,
> chocolate, yoghurt, but it didn't eat them. It made a nest by the
> back door but it wasn't happy and it was silent. I didn't know
> what to do. I asked my Mum and my Dad but they didn't know
> what to do. They didn't come to see it! Then I took it back to the
> edge of the big forest and I said, Go on! Go home!' And it walked
> into the forest and disappeared.

IN CLASS

1 Begin the lesson by drawing a small dragon on the board.
   Don't tell the children what you are doing—this will increase
   the mystery and their involvement. Don't refer to the text.

   Here is a sketch you might like to use for the dragon:

Draw the circle first!

2 Ask the children to look at the text and to guess which word
   might describe the animal. If they don't know and can't guess
   then say they word 'dragon' and ask a child to point to the
   word in the text.
3 Continue drawing to illustrate garden, house, back door, big
   forest.
4 Now settle the children down into a 'story frame of mind'
   (you might ask them to close their eyes). Read the story to
   them slowly and quietly.

5 Tell the children that stories can be 'mothers' to new stories. Ask them to tell you the names of other creatures and agree on one to substitute for the dragon so than adventure can happen to it instead of the dragon!

6 Now work through the story, asking the children to suggest how the story might be changed by substituting words.

Here is an example of a new story with alternative words and phrases shown in bold type.

> I found a **golden bird** in the **cupboard**. I think it came from the **top of a mountain**. It was **small and thin** and there were **curly feathers** on its **neck**. I gave it many things, but it didn't eat them. It **sang in the bathroom** but it wasn't happy and it **cried**. I didn't know what to do. I asked my **big sister** but **she** didn't know what to do. **She** didn't come to see it! Then I took it to the **window** and I said, 'Go on! Go home!' And it **flew into the night** and disappeared.

Suggest that the children see if the original story can 'mother' more stories. Minimize the occurrence of grammatical changes by asking the children to change only the same words as were changed the first time.

Acknowledgements
The storyline was inspired by a poem by Brian Patten called
'The small dragon'.

3.2 Tall story retelling

A 'tall story' is a story in which the information is so exaggerated
as to be incredible.

LEVEL	**Pre-intermediate**
LANGUAGE	**Simple past tense; intensive listening and speaking**
TIME	**20–30 minutes**
MATERIALS	One small slip of paper or card for each child.
IN CLASS	1 Tell the children a tall story. For example:

I'm very tired! I'm very, very tired! (Yawn very obviously.)
Write this sentence pattern on the board to guide the children.

This morning	I read	three books.
	I ate	a packet of cornflakes and twenty eggs.
	I ran	twenty miles.
	I found	a hundred dollars.
	I fell	in the river.
	I flew	in the sky.

2 Each child writes his or her name on a small piece of paper.

They then think of a one-sentence 'tall story' describing
something which (could have) happened to them that morning.
They can write it down or just remember it. For example:

This morning I ate a packet of cornflakes and twenty eggs.
This morning I ran twenty miles.
This morning I found a hundred dollars.

3 The children now find a partner and tell their tall story to the other child. When they have done so, they give their partner the paper with their name on it.

4 The children then form new pairs. Each child must now pass on the tall story he or she has just learnt from their first partner. He or she must say who told the tall story and pass on the paper with his or her name on it:

This morning, Olga found a hundred dollars.

5 Allow five to ten minutes for all the stories to be passed on at least three or four times.

6 All the children sit down in their places and you help them to summarize the morning with astonishment!

What a morning! Olga found two hundred dollars! Brian fell in the river! Harriet flew in the sky! Johnny ate a packet of cornflakes and twenty eggs!

FOLLOW-UP

A natural extension of this activity would be for the children to write an extended tall story (rather than a single line). It is most profitable for them to work in pairs on this writing. Of course, they must be published! See Chapter 8 for making books.

VARIATION

You and the children write a description of a very ordinary morning on the board. For example:

This morning I woke up at seven o'clock. I got out of bed and I put on my clothes and went downstairs into the kitchen. I ate cornflakes for breakfast then I put on my coat and went to school. In the town I saw buses, cars, and a lot of people.

Now show the children how they can change this story:

This morning I woke up at three o'clock. I got out of the cupboard and I put on my goldfish and went upstairs to the supermarket. I ate cushions for breakfast then I put on a bottle of milk and went to Africa. In the bottle I saw monkeys, parrots, and a lot of pens.

Ask the children to make up their own totally tall story!

3.3 Mime a journey

LEVEL

Elementary and above

LANGUAGE

Fluency in listening and speaking

TIME

30 minutes

MATERIALS

A tape recorder, microphone, and cassette

PREPARATION

1 Preferably make an open space in the classroom, or use the aisles between the desks.

2 Make sure you can remember a story which the children can mime easily. Here is an example for you to use:

The walk

Wave 'Goodbye' to your mother.

Walk along the road. Stop. There is a gate.

Open the gate, go through the gate, and close it.

Walk in the wood. It is very quiet. Walk quietly. Look to the right and look to the left.

Stop and listen. Look to the right. Look to the left. Look behind you.

Now walk slowly. Look to the right and to the left.

Suddenly, you see a big wall. It is very high and very long.

Walk to the wall. There is a small door in the wall. Knock on the door. Wait. Knock again. Wait.

Open the door and put your head through the gap. You see a room, a big room. Look.

Go into the room. Stop! Look to the right. Look to the left. Listen.

Walk across the room very slowly and quietly. Walk around a big box in the middle of the room. Stop. Open the box, slowly. The lid is very heavy.

It is dark in the box. Look! Amazing!

Stop! What can you hear? Listen—someone is coming! A man or a woman? Or a monster?

Run! Go through the door! Close the door! Run through the wood. Don't hit the trees! Run to the left and then to the right and then to the left.

Open and close the gate. Run up the road to your house.

Open the door, go in the house, close the door, and sit down!

Another good story to use is 'The little Indian boy' in *Storytelling with Children* (page 84).

IN CLASS

1 In the first Steps of this activity you don't speak at all. Mime that the children should sit around you in a big circle.

2 Mime the story as slowly and as clearly as you can.

3 Now you can speak. Ask the children what they think the story was. You can help them by miming each part again.

4 Now ask the children to stand in the circle with you and to mime the story with you.

5 Sit down, but ask the children to stay standing within the circle of chairs. Tell the story and ask the children to mime it as they hear you tell it.

6 Tell the children to sit in a circle or semicircle. Put the tape recorder in the circle.

7 Switch the tape recorder on and set it with the pause button. Start the story. For example, you might say:

I left my house and said 'Goodbye' to my mother.

8 Explain that you want the class to retell the story and that you will help them to get the sentences right before you record what they say. Only record a child when he or she can say the next sentence correctly. For example:

Child 1:	*I walk ... road.*
You:	*I walked along the road.*
Child 1:	*I walked along the road. (record)*
Child 2:	*There was a gate. I went through the gate.*
You:	*Good! Now let's record it!*

COMMENTS

1 By using the pause button you finish up with a recording of the story without any mistakes of content or language.

2 With lower-proficiency children accept even a single word and then offer them a sentence with the word in the present tense. Be consistent in your use of the past or present tense.

With higher-proficiency children you can ask them to describe the gate and the wood and the wall and door. And you can ask the children to tell you their different ideas for what might have been in the box.

FOLLOW-UP

Pairs or groups of children can invent another mime story. Ask them to do it for the class.

Acknowledgements

I first saw the basis of this idea in: Baudains, R. and M. Baudains. 1990. *Alternatives.* Harlow: Longman.

3.4 Your pictures and mime

LEVEL

Elementary and above

LANGUAGE

Present tense; fluency in listening and speaking

TIME

20–30 minutes

PREPARATION

Learn a very short story and be able to sketch it. You can use the story on page 61, which is one of Aesop's fables.

IN CLASS

1 You draw six sketches on the board quickly. After each sketch, mime any part of the story which will help the children's understanding. The children guess and call out their ideas. You remain silent. You can write the key vocabulary next to the appropriate part of the sketch, for example, the gnat.

2 The children can then try to retell the story, prompted by the pictures.

1 This is a gnat. This is a lion. The lion is the king of the jungle.

2 The gnat doesn't like the lion. He bites the lion's nose.

3 The lion is very angry. He wants to bite the gnat.

4 The lion can't bite the gnat. The gnat is very small. The gnat laughs.

5 The gnat tells the crocodile, and the elephant and the monkey, 'I am the winner!'

6 Then the gnat flies into a spider's web. The spider kills the gnat and eats it.

4 Beginnings and endings

This chapter concentrates on activities where children are given the beginning or ending of a story and have to use their imagination to complete it, either orally or in writing.

the children add the beginning or ending

or add to a story and pass it on

4.1 Three-quarters of a story

LEVEL

Pre-intermediate

LANGUAGE

Written fluency

TIME

30–40 minutes

IN CLASS

Give the children three-quarters of a story and ask them to finish it.

VARIATIONS

Even this well-known activity can be done in two very different ways:

1 Predicting the author's finish

Tell the children they must do their best to write the missing part of the story exactly as the author probably wrote it. This is intellectually demanding and there is an ultimate right or wrong answer, when you produce the actual ending.

2 Creating an alternative ending

Ask the children to write the most interesting (amusing, provocative, exciting) ending they can to complete the story. This demands creativity and there can be no right or wrong. The class can decide who has produced the best ending—the author or one of them!

4.2 First line and write a paragraph

LEVEL   **Pre-intermediate**

LANGUAGE   **Written fluency**

TIME   **30–40 minutes**

PREPARATION   Write the sentences below onto strips of card or paper big
enough for the class to use. Modify the sentences if you think
they are too difficult for your children, but they do not need to
understand every word.

The little cat walks in the wood. 'Where am I?' she says.
The giant is hungry and there is no food in the cupboard.
Sheriff Hank Coldfinger is tired but he can't sleep; the town of Tombstone is too quiet.
The little Christmas tree knows it is nearly Christmas.
I was born in a small village near Edinburgh in 1785.
Helen can't run and she can't swim but she can think!
A small green hand opened the door and three eyes on sausages looked into the room.
He lay absolutely still; the police were just outside the door.
'Goal!' the crowd shouted but Alan lay on the mud; he didn't move.

Photocopiable © Oxford University Press

IN CLASS   1 Put the sentence strips on the board one by one. Ask the
children to read each strip aloud and to say what kind of
story might follow. You can say themes for them to choose
from, or write them on the board. (In this case, they are:
animal story, fairy story, cowboy story, Christmas story,
historical story, adventure, science fiction, crime, and
sport.)
2 Tell the children that they are going to write the first
paragraph of a story based on one of the sentences. Let the
class choose one sentence and see if they can put a paragraph
together orally.

3 Each child chooses one of the other sentences and writes a first paragraph. They should write the first line at the top of a piece of paper and then fold it back. They must leave space at the bottom of the paper. They must not tell their neighbour which sentence they have chosen.

> Sherriff Hank Coldfinger is tired but he can't sleep; the town of Tombstone is too quiet!
>
> Coldfinger walks quietly in the street. It is dark. There is no moon. He looks through the windows of the houses. He listens. Nothing!

4 Give the children ten minutes to write a paragraph 20 to 30 words long. Stop them all at the same time and ask them to exchange their paragraph with their neighbour.

5 They read their neighbour's paragraph and write down the first line they think their neighbour has chosen.

6 They now unfold the first line.

FOLLOW-UPS

– Write more first paragraphs based on different first lines.
– Display paragraphs based on the same first line together.
– The children try to write first lines of their own.
– First paragraphs are passed to other children to write a middle story paragraph and then to other children to write the last paragraph.

VARIATION

1 The children work in groups of five or six. Give each group the same sentence to start a story. The groups have exactly fifteen minutes to invent a story. There must be as many parts to the story as there are children in the group.

2 Each child must learn and remember one part of the story. The group makes sure that each child can remember his or her part of the story.

3 Each group 'performs' their story for the rest of the class. The children not speaking can provide a Greek chorus of vocal noises and comment.

4.3 Crazy start and crazy finish

LEVEL   **Pre-intermediate**

LANGUAGE   **Oral and written fluency**

TIME   **20–30 minutes**

IN CLASS
1 Write this paragraph on the board:

   It was a cold winter's night. The parrot was eating newspapers and the huge turtles were asleep. Suddenly Hubert heard a noise. What was it? Was it a dog? Was it a car?

2 Ask the children to read the paragraph and make sure they understand it. Agree that it is a crazy paragraph.

3 Now challenge the children to invent a second paragraph which, in some way, finishes the story and makes it almost sensible! For example:

   Hubert opened the door. He looked into the forest and saw a car. A dog got out of the car and ran into the house. The dog was very angry—the parrot was eating his newspapers!

4 Tell the children to work in pairs and to write a crazy first paragraph. Give them exactly five minutes to do this.

5 They exchange their first paragraphs with another pair and then add another paragraph to make the first paragraph seem almost reasonable.

6 They pass their crazy stories to the other children to read.

FOLLOW-UP   If the activity has been successful then make posters or books of the stories. The opportunity for illustration is rich!

VARIATION 1   Give a crazy final paragraph to the children and ask them to write the first paragraph. Here is an example:

   The giant was tired. He got into the cupboard and he slept and he slept. The mouse said, 'You can go now!' So they picked up the little box and went home.

VARIATION 2   The children have the first and the last parts and must write the part in the middle.

COMMENTS   This activity aims to liberate the children's fantasy.

Acknowledgments
I found the original idea in *Impro* by Keith Johnson (see Further Reading).

4.4 Domino stories

LEVEL

Pre-intermediate

LANGUAGE

Oral fluency

TIME

30–40 minutes

PREPARATION

Photocopy and cut up five small picture cards for each child.

IN CLASS

1 Arrange children into groups of four or five. Give each child five picture cards.
2 One child puts down a card and begins a story, referring to the picture.
3 The next child puts down a card and tries to continue the same story, referring to his or her own picture.
4 When all the cards are down the groups make sure everyone in the group can retell the whole story.

FOLLOW-UP

1 One child from each group moves to another group and tells the story to them.
2 Then a different child tries to remember the story and passes it on to the next group. This continues until the story has been passed through about three or four storytellers.
3 Finally the children return to their original groups, who listen to the story in its third or fourth version. They see if it has changed.

VARIATION 1

Any information can put on the card, including single words, phrases, symbols, and so on.

VARIATION 2

Include a 'joker' in each pack with a magic wand which can be used to mean anything.

VARIATION 3

1 The children work in groups of four to six. Each group has about twelve small pictures placed upside down on their table (there are useful pictures at the back of *Storytelling with Children*). Each child in succession turns over any four pictures and tries to make a story connection between them. For example, this *dog* is eating this *pilot's sausage* in his *car*.
2 The child then replaces the pictures face down again and the next child turns over any four pictures to continue the story.

4.5 One-sentence starter

LEVEL   **Elementary and above**

LANGUAGE   **Fluency with a focus on writing**

TIME   **30–40 minutes**

IN CLASS   1 The children work in groups of five or six. Each group is given the same sentence as a start to a story. The groups have exactly fifteen minutes to invent a story. There must be as many parts to the story as there are children in the group.

2 Each child must learn and remember one part of the story. The group makes sure that each child can remember his or her part of the story.

3 Each group 'performs' their story for the rest of the class. The children who are not speaking can provide a 'Greek chorus' of vocal noises and comment.

4.6 Pass the story (oral)

LEVEL   **Elementary and above**

LANGUAGE   **Simple past tense, oral fluency**

TIME   **15–20 minutes**

PREPARATION   1 It is important to warm the children up thoroughly and get them into a story-making frame of mind (for instance, by using some of the 'story warmers' in Chapter 1) as some children can find it quite daunting to have to improvise a story in English.

2 You can make it easier linguistically by giving or revising key vocabulary beforehand.

IN CLASS   1 You begin a story and one of the children continues it. For example, you might start the story by saying:

Last night I opened my cupboard door and I saw a very, very small mouse.

A child might continue the story by adding:

I said 'Hello' to the mouse and the mouse said 'Hello' to me.

2 Each child in the class adds something to the story.

VARIATIONS   There are various ways of prompting children to continue the story:
- in order of the way they are sitting—you might have them sitting in a circle
- volunteers
- the child telling the story throws a paper ball to the next child
- move to another child after a single sentence or when somebody (not necessarily you) claps
- before the story begins give each child a number on a card— the children continue the story according to the number they have
- a pile of pictures is passed around a circle of children and music is played. When the music stops the child with the cards must try to continue the story by referring to the picture on the top. He or she then puts the picture at the bottom of the pack and the music starts again
- a child deliberately stops his or her contribution halfway through a sentence or with the word 'and'
- any child can say 'Pass!'

There are also various ways of influencing the content of what the children say:
- let them say whatever they wish
- give each child a word or phrase before the story begins and tell them they must use it in their contribution to the story (an opportunity to practise your current language teaching point!)

– give each child a picture and ask them to stand in line with
their picture when they add to the story.
– use dialogue instead of narrative form
– each child adds only one word:

*Once ... a ... dog ... came ... out ... of ... his ... house ... He ...
was ... big ... but ... he ... was ... not ... brave*

4.7 Pass the story (written)

LEVEL	**Pre-intermediate**
LANGUAGE	**Simple past tense, written fluency**
TIME	**40 minutes**
MATERIALS	A piece of paper for each child about 20 cm x 30 cm
IN CLASS	1 Every child writes the opening sentence of a story on a piece of paper.
	2 After exactly three minutes they pass the story in one direction to the neighbouring child. The children read what their neighbour has written and then add to the story. Give them four minutes to read the story so far and add their own sentence.
	3 The stories pass along seven or eight children before being returned to the originators. In this way every child receives back a story which he or she began.
VARIATIONS	– the children work in pairs, passing the two stories between them
	– the children have a word, a phrase, a picture, or an object on their desks. They must begin their story by referring to it and then continue every story that comes to them by referring to it as well
	– instead of a narrative style, the children write the whole story in dialogue form, and perform it at the end
	– each child writes a line of a story and then folds it over so that the next child cannot see it. In the traditional game 'consequences', the story is set and each child writes only one or two words:

[boy] *met* [girl] *at* [place]. *He said ... She said ... And the
consequence was ...*

FOLLOW-UP	On receiving back the story they began, the children check through all the contributions and try to correct any errors they find. They discuss the mistakes and corrections with each contributor. Any disputes can be brought to you.

4.8 Dialogue with a dragon

LEVEL	**Pre-intermediate**
LANGUAGE	**Fluency in all four skills**
TIME	**30–40 minutes**
IN CLASS	1 Tell the children that you are going to go into a story with them. Tell the children that they must be very quiet because they must leave the classroom and go into a forest.

1 Tell the children that you are going to go into a story with them. Tell the children that they must be very quiet because they must leave the classroom and go into a forest.

2 Explain that the story is about two people and a dragon in the forest. Divide the children into groups of three with one child as the dragon. If there is one child extra, one group can have two dragons. If there are two children extra let them be a pair: one dragon and one person.

3 Make sure they know the following words: *forest, branch, twig, trunk, stick, magic wand, dragon, dark, frightened.* You can use the drawing on the next page. Show 'dark' by peering about as if you can't see very well. Show 'frightened' by shaking and pretending to bite your finger nails.

4 Now the children must be very quiet. If they like they can put their heads on their arms on their desks, and close their eyes.

5 Begin the story:

Now, dragons: you are lying in the middle of the forest. You are not asleep but your eyes are closed. You are thinking. Lie very still.

Now the two people: you are walking in the forest. You are walking between the trees. You are walking on soft ground. You don't want to make a noise. You stop for a moment. Look around you at the trees. Look up. Can you see the sky? It is very quiet and it is a little bit dark, not very dark but a little bit. You walk on, quietly, between the trees. You think there is something special in the forest today. You feel a little bit frightened, not very frightened but a little bit. You look at your friend but you don't speak.

Then you find two magic wands on the ground. You think they are sticks but they aren't. They are magic wands. You pick them up.

Suddenly you hear a noise! What can it be? And then you see something! What can it be? It's a dragon? Have a look at the dragon. What do you feel about it?

Dragon! You hear a noise. You open your eyes and you see two people! What do you think? What do you feel? Now all of you: open your eyes, slowly, slowly. Please don't speak for a moment or two.

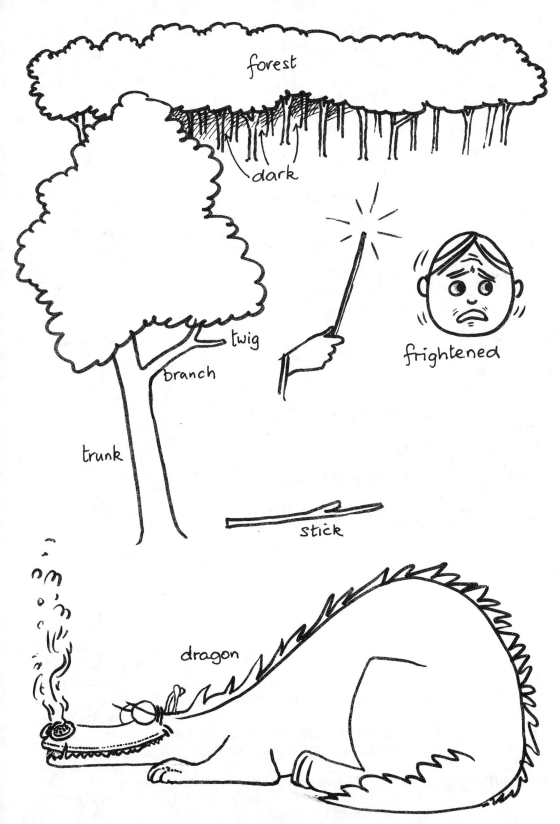

forest

dark

twig

branch

trunk

frightened

stick

dragon

6 While the children are slowly coming back into the classroom,
begin to write on the board:

Dragon:
First person:
Dragon:
Second person:
First person:
Dragon:
Both people:
Dragon:

The children will see you doing this and will begin to realize
what you want them to do. Explain that you want them to write
down what they each say. They must learn their parts and then
act it out for another group or perhaps for the whole class.

COMMENTS

The number of exchanges depends on the children's proficiency
level and involvement. However, all the groups must finish about
the same time.

FOLLOW-UP

Of course, if the children are sufficiently interested this would
make a very nice book.

4.9 Two-month class saga

LEVEL

Elementary

LANGUAGE

Simple past tense

TIME

**Almost no lesson time and only homework time by
individual children**

IN CLASS

1 Start a story by writing down the first sentence:

Once upon a time there was an old man.

At the end of each lesson, the children decide among
themselves which child has worked best in class that day. This
child takes the story home to add one more sentence. The
story is secret for everyone before they deserve to take it home.

2 Carry on for about two months. The children take home a
draft copy to add to, and you make a clean, corrected copy.
The clean copy is taken away only for illustration.

3 At the end of two months, when the story is developing
towards an end, photocopy the pages for all the children and
ask them to finish it as they like.

COMMENTS

1 The children have a sense of creating a 'group product' and
value each other's contributions, but are also motivated to
work hard individually.

2 The group becomes more and more reliable at judging their class performance and at choosing which child should take the story home.

Acknowledgements
This activity was contributed by Agnes Enyedi, Hungary. She made a story with her whole class (ten- to twelve-year-olds), mainly in their homework time. 'I did it to encourage writing, creativity, and working together. And, by the way, every child contributed!'

5 Filling in and filling out

In this family of activities, the children have a sequence of 'bits of information' which cue their story-making. The bits of information can be anything: single words or longer texts to copy, complete, write as a dictation, or expand; pictures drawn by the children or from magazines; abstract pictures; maps, music, non-verbal sounds on tape, food, drink, objects to feel—anything!

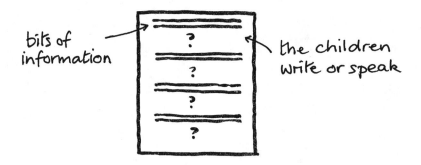

The sequence can be random or structured.

Structured sequence

The sequence of information helps the child to construct the story in an ordered way. You can present each bit of information in order and explain what it represents:

This picture shows the main person.
This letter shows his problem.
This music gives you a feeling for where he is and how he feels.

Random sequence

If the bits of information are presented with no particular idea of a sequence, the children are responsible for inventing one for themselves.

5.1 Build your story

LEVEL	Elementary and above
LANGUAGE	Listening, selecting, retaining, retelling, reading and writing
TIME	20–30 minutes
PREPARATION	Make four photocopies of the text below (more for a big class) or adapt it to the language the children have learnt.

It is a dark night.
It is raining.
It is snowing.
It is sunny.
The wind is blowing, it is raining, and it is dark.

The little boy runs down the street.
The little girl walks through the wood.
The old woman sleeps in front of the fire.
The old man reads his book.
The king cries.
The fisherman dreams.
The parrot flies.

Suddenly he sees a big dog.
Suddenly there is a loud bang!
Suddenly a crocodile comes.
Suddenly a big, black bird flies in front of the moon.

He is frightened.
She is very happy!
He is very surprised.
She says, 'Oh, no! Oh, no!'
He says, 'You are very nice!'
It says, 'I'm hungry'.
He says, 'What's that?'
She says, 'What can I do?'

She says, 'Goodbye'.
He says, 'See you later'.
He says, 'I'm going home!'
It says, 'You are not eating me!'
They smile.
They laugh.
They go home. They play together.

IN CLASS

1 Put the copies of the text on the walls where the children can stand to read each of them.

2 Ask the children to go and read them through. Check that they understand all the vocabulary.

3 Tell the children they are going to use the sentences to make a story. Read out the first set of sentences and ask them to listen for the one they would like to start their story with. Ask a few children to tell you which sentence they have chosen. Get them to say it several times. Praise them. Read the sentences again for the children who have not yet chosen one.

4 Do the same with each of the sets of sentences. Don't let them write down anything yet.

5 When you have been through all the sets of sentences and checked that most children seem to be choosing one from each set, tell them that they can now go to the sentences on the wall and copy down the sentences they have chosen. However, insist that they do not copy the sentences in front of the texts but only when they get back to their tables. This makes them internalize the sentence as a whole unit. They can keep on returning to the text several times for each sentence, if they need to.

6 Here are some guidelines or rules you can give them:
   – They must make a story.
   – They can change the sentences if they wish, for example, change 'he' to 'she'.
   – They can take more than one sentence from each set if they wish.
   – They can add extra information if they like.

VARIATION

When the class are used to the technique, you and the children can brainstorm other sentences of your own. That would be more fun and provide much more language development for the children.

5.2 Clothes line story

LEVEL

Elementary and above for the class oral production
Pre-intermediate for the written story

LANGUAGE

Oral fluency followed by written fluency and accuracy, using language resources to the full

TIME

One hour to get the clothes line up and all the things on it plus getting the story started. Another 30 minutes to get the story finished in first draft.

MATERIALS

A clothes line long enough to go from one side of the classroom to the other (or across a corner), clothes pegs or bulldog clips, thick pens, things to hang from the line, small pieces of paper for the children to write and draw on, magazine pictures, chocolate wrappings, a cap, money, toys, a bag, bits of cloth, a twig from a tree, a sock—anything at all.

PREPARATION

Work out how you are going to fix the clothes line across the classroom before you embark on this activity!

IN CLASS

1 Ideally, fix the line when the children are in the class (make sure you know how to do it beforehand).

2 Explain to them, in a tantalizing way, that it is a story clothes line. Let them see you put lots of pegs on it—some children can help you to do this.

3 Put a big piece of paper on the board and ask who would like to be the artist for the story. Ask the child to stand by the paper but only to draw what the other children tell him or her. The other children, with your guidance, describe the appearance of the main person who is to be in the story. (Make sure the artist draws on a really big scale.)

4 Let the class decide who this person is (name, age, what he/she likes, etc.).

5 Clip the drawing of the person to the clothes line.

6 Give every child a piece of paper and ask them to write a word or a sentence, or to do a drawing on it. Ask the children to make their words and pictures big enough to be seen easily (thick pens are useful).

7 As they are finished hang the words and pictures on the line. If there are too many to fit on, use sticky tape to join them together so that they hang down in a ladder arrangement.

8 Now invite the children to think of other things they could hang on the line. These should be hung between the various words and drawings. (With lower-proficiency learners it might be easier for them to have fewer things hanging on the line.)

As this is being done, keep talking about how the various

things could be used in the story so that the children will realize that the story is going to be made out of all the pieces.

9   With beginners, make a story with the whole class. With more proficient children, ask them to work in pairs and to write their way along the washing line, making use of as many different things as they can.

10 When two pairs of children have finished their story then ask them to exchange stories. They should now try to read the other pair's story and work out what they were referring to on the washing line.

VARIATION

If you have your own classroom, you can fit a wire along the top of the board and hang cards, pictures, and other things. on it. You will find the wire useful for all kinds of other activities, for example, spelling and word order.

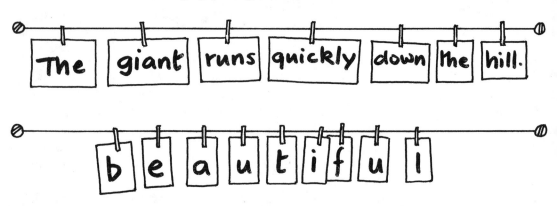

COMMENTS

1   The washing line and the contribution by all the children creates an atmosphere of fun, invention, and class co-operation.

2   The clothes line represents the linear arrangement of ideas within a story and can also be used to demonstrate the ideas in Chapter 6, 'Sorting and sequencing'. See also page 2.9.

3   Extra information can be hung underneath the main piece, for example, a magazine photo may represent the main protagonist, and various other pictures representing things that are important to him or her could hang underneath.

5.3 A fairy tale with holes in it

LEVEL

Elementary

LANGUAGE

Mainly writing, simple past tense but with a lot of help

TIME

2 hours

MATERIALS

A piece of paper for each child

PREPARATION

1 It is helpful if the children have been studying fairy tales in their mother tongue.

2 In a previous lesson, the children make large fairy tale characters to decorate the walls (for example, a king, a queen, dragons, giants, and witches).

3 Make a photocopy of the 'fairy tale with holes in it' and the word list for each child.

IN CLASS

1 In the children's first language, ask what the characters are called in English.

2 Give each child a copy of the 'fairy tale with holes in it' and the first word list.

3 Go through the 'fairy tale with holes in it' together hole by hole, looking at the various ways in which the words could be put into the 'holes'. The class agree on their choice. The story can be as crazy as they like (for example, we had a rather grotesque and very funny story about a dragon who met a teacher and was given an elephant which he put in his pocket!).

4 The children are now ready to write their own fairy tales. Give them all a sheet of paper.

5 Put all the stories together to make a book. Make lots of copies so that each child can take one home, plus more to show people.

Fairy tale with holes in it

(The numbers refer to the lists of alternative words.)

Once upon a time there was a/an (1) _____ (2) _____

who lived in a/an (3) _____ (4) _____

He/she was very unhappy, because (5) _____

Then one day he/she met a/an (6) _____ (7) _____

who said to him/her: 'Can I help you?' 'Yes, please,' said the

(2) _____ The (7) _____ gave him/her

(8) _____ and said: (9) _____

The (2) _____ did what the (7) _____ said, and the next morning (10) _____

Now the (2) _____ was very happy/sad and (12) _____

lived happily ever after.

Word lists

1	2	3	4
young	prince	big	house
old	princess	small	castle
clever	king	dark	forest
ugly	queen	black	cave
rich	witch	white	cabin
poor	giant	blue	caravan
little	boy	red	tent
stupid	girl		
beautiful	dragon		

5	6
he/she had no money	big
he/she had no friends	friendly
he/she had to go to school	happy
he/she was very fat	green
he/she had a long nose	dirty
his/her bike had been stolen	tall
it was always raining	thin
he/she could not find his/her glasses	strong

7	8	9
monster	a red apple	'Put it in your pocket.'
cat	a big ice-cream	'Take it to school with you.'
girl	a green sweater	'Eat it for dinner.'
boy	a spaceship	'Give it to your mother.'
frog	a pencil case	'Throw it in the swimming pool.'
teacher	a pink rose	'Send it to a school in Denmark.'
truck driver	a walkman	'Fly over the ocean with it.'
shop assistant	an elephant	

10
the sun was shining
he/she had turned into a dragon
he/she found a box full of gold
he/she had a stomach-ache
he/she did not know where he/she was
he/she had become very thin
he/she found a car at his/her bedside
he/she had a lot of new friends

11	12
went to live in Denmark	he
went to bed	she
drowned himself/herself in the swimming pool	the (2)
drank a whole bottle of whisky	the (7)
married the (7)	they both
never went to school again	they all
invited all his friends to a party	nobody

Example

This is the first story in Hanne Pedersen's class storybook:

Once upon a time there was a little dragon who lived in a big castle.
He was very unhappy because he had become very thin. One day
he met the princess and ate her for dinner but the princess was
poison and the dragon died.

VARIATION 1

If you have an overhead projector, at step 2 only give the
children the text. Copy the word list onto transparencies and cut
them up. Put the text on to the overhead projector together with
the word list for the first hole. The whole class decides on the
best word. Continue like this until all the holes are filled.

If you do not have an overhead projector you can write the text
and words on the board.

VARIATION 2

If they prefer, the children can follow the 'fairy tale with holes in
it' and use only the words on the word list sheet. Other children
may prefer to ask for new words and not follow the 'fairy tale
with holes in it' text at all.

COMMENTS

If you do not give the children all the word lists at once, you can
keep a certain amount of suspense until the end of the story,
which keeps their attention.

Acknowledgements
This example of a gapped story was devised by Hanne L.
Pedersen in Denmark for her class of eleven-year-olds in their
second year of English.

5.4 Bare bones story

You tell a very simple story and the children ask questions to make it richer and more interesting.

LEVEL	**Elementary**
LANGUAGE	**Questions, listening and speaking fluency**
TIME	**20–30 minutes**

PREPARATION   You might like to have ideas ready for the box in the story:

small   size of a cup   round   lid doesn't open
very heavy   dark blue colour with stars on it
he cannot open it but he wants it
inside is space or another world or other worlds

IN CLASS

1 Write on the board *The man walks along the road.*
2 Ask the children questions about this sentence so that they begin to make a richer story. They must invent answers to your questions. (This will show the children how to ask you questions later.)

Examples
Who is this man? What is his name? What is his job?
What does he look like?
Why is he walking along the road? Where is he going?
How is he walking? Slowly, quickly?
Where is the road?
What time is it? What is the weather like?

Write the questions on the board if you think it will help the children to ask questions in the next step.

3 Begin telling the story, including as much as possible of what the children have suggested. Here is an example using words and phrases which second-year children might have contributed (the teacher has contributed the full sentences and the grammar and syntax):

The old man walked slowly along the road. It was snowing and it was dark, and Mr Bennet was going home. Midnight! It was very late for Mr Bennet but he could not walk quickly. He had a bad heart and weak knees and his bag was very heavy.

4 Write on the board box. Tell the children that they must ask you as many questions as they can think of to link the box with the man. Guide them into creating a story where the old man has a desire/wish/want/need/aim (or series of these) but meets difficulties in achieving it/them. When his desires have been resolved one way or another (and no more unfulfilled desires have been introduced!) the story is over. (See Chapter 2, page 33).

VARIATION 1   Instead of switching the questioning role to the children halfway through, keep the questioning role for yourself the first time you do the activity.

VARIATION 2   You tell the story, but keep on stopping to say you do not know anything more about the thing you have referred to. For example:

You:	*Once upon a time there was a man. But I don't know anything about the man.*
Children:	(calling out): *He was old. He was strong. He was rich.*
You:	*Once upon a time there was a man. He was old and strong and rich. One day ... but I don't know anything about the day.*
Children:	*It was Tuesday. It was sunny.*
You:	*One day, it was a Tuesday and it was sunny, the old man looked for his little cat. But I don't know anything about the little cat ...*

In this example the teacher introduces the problem; the questions and the children's answers will eventually find the cat and the story will end happily. A child might be able to take over your role.

VARIATION 3   Do the activity in written form. Give the children a 'bare bones text' such as:

A girl looks for her cat. She asks, 'Where is my cat?'. She finds it.

The children expand the story. You might give them useful words and phrases.

If the children like bare bones texts, ask them to write them for each other.F

VARIATION 4   Point the children's imaginations in a general direction but do not give any detail. The children write down their ideas or tell them to their neighbour.

Example

You:	*You are walking along a path. Is it a wide or a narrow path?*
Children:	*(write their ideas or tell their neighbour)*
You:	*How do you feel?*
Children:	*(write their ideas or tell their neighbour)*
You:	*You find a key. Is it big or small? Is it old or new? Do you keep it?*
Children:	*(write their ideas or tell their neighbour)*

VARIATION 5   Use a flowchart to create a 'bare bones' story (see 2.10, 'Three-part flowchart story').

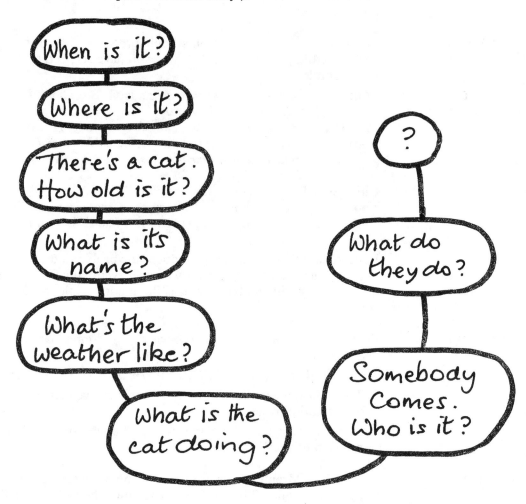

5.5 A crazy play

LEVEL   Elementary

LANGUAGE   Listening for detail

TIME   20–30 minutes

PREPARATION   1 Prepare small pieces or strips of paper—enough for one per child but at least 16.

2 Make a place where the prince can sleep, for example, a table.

IN CLASS   1 Give every child a strip of paper. Tell them to write on their strip of paper any sentence which someone might say. They should remember what they have written.

2 Write these words on the board:

king, queen, prince, princess, monster, crowds of people.

Tell the children that you want them to put on a play in the class and you need five volunteers to take the parts of the main characters. Everybody else can be the crowd of people.

3 Collect the sentences from the class and give each child actor some of them. You need at least the following amounts: king (3), queen (4), prince (3), princess (3), monster (3)—total 16. You can give them more so that they can choose which to say.

4 Establish the court scene first. For example, say:

This table is the prince's bed. These two chairs are the thrones for the king and queen.

Tell the story, moving the actors. Every so often indicate that they should read out one of their sentences. When you refer to the crowd of people, all the class must say the sentences they originally wrote. Of course the sentences are random and this often makes them very funny.

The sleeping prince

Once upon a time there was a prince who was asleep. He slept and he slept and he slept, day after day and week after week. Everybody was very worried. The king said, ... and the queen said, ... The crowd of people said ...

Sometimes the prince spoke. One day he said, ... and his mother said, ... But he slept and he slept and he slept!

They poured cold water on him. They hit his feet. They shouted at him. The king shouted ... The queen shouted ... The princess shouted ... and the crowd of people shouted ... But it was no good! The prince didn't wake up.

One day the king said, ... and the queen said, ...

So, at last, the princess, his sister said, ...

And the princess left the castle and she walked and walked and walked until she came to a big mountain. She climbed the big mountain. She climbed and she climbed and she climbed. At last she came to a cave. In the cave there was a monster. She said, ... and the monster said, ...

Then the monster walked down the mountain to the castle. He went into the castle and he said, ...

The prince woke up and said, ... and then he said, ...
The king said, ...
The queen said, ...
The princess said, ...
The monster said, ...
The crowd of people said, ...

Acknowledgements

I think I learnt this idea from Jim Wingate.

5.6 Question stories

LEVEL

Near-beginners and above (depending on the questions you ask)

LANGUAGE

Listening fluency plus some oral practice

TIME

25–35 minutes

PREPARATION

Before the children come into the room, place the chairs in a rectangle or U-shape. This is essential; the special arrangement helps to put the children into a special frame of mind.

IN CLASS

1 Tell the children that they are going to make a story. They have exactly twenty-five minutes. They do not have to speak, but if they say something and you hear it, it must be in the story. If two people say different things, then the different things must be in the story.

2 Now ask and gather the answers to the following questions (adapting them to the level of your children):

Who is in your story?
Is it a man or a woman, a boy or a girl, or an aminal?
How old is he/she?
What's his/her name?
Where does your story begin?

Make them be precise. If they say America, get them to say exactly where. For example: *In a café in New York. In a corner of the café. She is sitting near a window.*

When does your story begin?

If necessary, give them a choice of words, for example: *Monday, Tuesday, winter, spring, morning, afternoon*, etc.

What is the weather like?

3 Repeat the description as it builds up. Do not select and do not let anyone try to reject anyone else's suggestion. Everything you hear must be in the story. If some of the information is contradictory, ask the class to sort it out but they must include both bits of information. For example, if one child says the girl is ten and another child says the girl is fifteen, they might say, 'Really she's ten, but she says she is fifteen'.

4 When you have got to the point where something must happen, ask:

Exactly what is ... doing at this moment?
What happens then?
What does he/she do, hear, think, feel, say?

Keep on repeating the story to the class from the beginning. This is wonderful listening fluency practice.

5 It is not your job to find an ending for the story, but it is your job to remind them of the time! For example: *You have got exactly four minutes left to finish your story. How are you going to do it?*

VARIATION 1

If the children really cannot think of anything to say, stop. In the next lesson retell the story as far as they have got. You can say, for example, *Is she still sitting in the corner of the café?*

VARIATION 2

Do not always follow the conventional order of who, where, when, and what. Give the children the experience of sequencing the elements of the story differently: for example, you might begin with the time and the place.

VARIATION 3

During the story-making you can stop to dramatize the story two or three times. Don't use any props even if you have them. Make rooms or houses out of about eight children holding hands. Make doors which open and close out of children with their arms outstretched. Children can be trees, bicycles, anything. In one story-making session in Hungary, one child held his hands over another child's ears because he was the other boy's walkman! You provide the narration of the story; the children act it and speak if they can.

VARIATION 4

1 Ask volunteer children to draw a picture for each question, for example: Who is in the story? What does she look like? Who is her friend? What is the weather like?

2 Collect the pictures and help the class to make a story with them, elaborating the ideas they have already invented and illustrated.

3 Put the pictures on the wall in the form of a picture strip.

FOLLOW-UP

The children write letters to each other as if they were characters in the story.

COMMENTS

1 The children learn how to make a story with the English they have rather than trying to think of a story in their mother tongue and then feeling the frustration of trying to translate it into English.

2 Never add anything to the story, not even 'very'! Remember that it is not your story but the children's. Of course, you may need to retell the story with full sentences.

Acknowledgements
The use of basic questions plus guidelines derives from the time when I worked with Word in Action (Dorset). I have also received guidance and inspiration from the work of Dorothy Heathcote (see Further Reading).

5.7 Crazy sentence pattern stories

LEVEL	**Elementary and above**
LANGUAGE	**Sentence patterns you wish to practise**
TIME	**20–40 minutes**
PREPARATION	Decide which patterns you wish to practise.
IN CLASS	1 Write on the board an example of a sentence pattern which you want the children to practise. Choose an example which is imaginative and likely to intrigue the children. For example: *Many years ago a boy was flying in the sky.*
	2 Tell the children that you want them to make lots of crazy sentences of a similar kind. Draw long vertical lines to divide the sentence into its constituent parts. As you do so, talk to the children about how the sentence is built.

Many years ago	a	boy girl snowman	was	flying swimming running sleeping	in the sky
	some two	U.F.O.'s sparrows	were		

3 Invite the children to suggest alternatives for *boy*. For example, *a girl, a man, a snowman, some UFOs, two sparrows.*

4 Invite the children to suggest alternatives for *flying*. For example, *swimming, running, eating, sleeping.*

5   Invite the children to find alternative adverbs of time and place: for example, *thousands of years ago, three years ago, last week; in space, outside the school, in the playground, at home.*

Thousands of years ago Three years ago Last week Many years ago	*a* *some* *two*	*boy* *girl* *snowman* *U.F.O.'s* *sparrows*	*was* *were*	*flying* *swimming* *running* *eating* *sleeping*	*in the sky* *in space* *outside the school* *in the playground* *at home*

6   Have some fun with the children making up funny combinations of words. Then say that they could make a story if they had a few more sentences.

7   Suggest a few more sentences and do the same with them. For example:

Suddenly a Martian shouted in the cupboard.
So the boy ran away.

Alternatives might be:

A few minutes later
And then
Girl, elephants
Jumped, laughed

9   Now enjoy making crazy stories with the children!

10 It may be enough to have the fun of inventing the stories. However, the children may well like to make some of them into books (see Chapter 8).

Acknowledgements
This activity derives from my work with Julia Dudás.

5.8 Three-picture story

LEVEL

Pre-intermediate

LANGUAGE

Fluency in all four skills

TIME

30 minutes

PREPARATION

1 Choose three magazine pictures. They must be big enough for the children to see. It also helps the stories if they are a little bit unusual.

2 Check that the children have enough vocabulary to say something about the pictures. Before beginning the activity you might like to show each picture and to brainstorm onto the board all the words and phrases they can say about it.

3 The children must have pens and paper ready.

IN CLASS

1 Tell the children they are going to write a story based on three pictures you are going to show them. They have four minutes exactly for the start of their story. Show them the first picture for a few seconds. They must start writing their story immediately.

2 After exactly four minutes stop the children writing, even if they are in the middle of a sentence. Tell them to take it in turns to read their story so far to their neighbour.

3 Ask two children, in turn, to read their stories to the class.

4 Show the children the second picture. Tell them to continue exactly the same story without any interruption to it.

5 After exactly four minutes stop the children and ask them to read the continuation of their story to the same neighbour.

6 Show the children the third picture. Tell them they must find a way of finishing their story in four minutes based on that picture.

7 Once more the children read their next instalment to their neighbour.

8 Ask the same two children as before to read out the final part of their stories.

VARIATION

The whole class can call out ideas for a class oral story.

COMMENTS

1 This is a powerful and easy-to-organize activity which does not need any follow-up. Of course, if the children want to improve and redraft their stories and to make a book of them, that is marvellous.

2 This activity provides fun in writing a story under pressure. It is interesting that a time and picture cue *restriction* can produce *creativity*.

Acknowledgements
This activity was inspired by Alan Maley and Alan Duff, *Drama Techniques in Language Learning* (see Further Reading).

5.9 Story on an island

LEVEL   **Pre-intermediate**

LANGUAGE   **Oral and written fluency**

TIME   **40–50 minutes**

PREPARATION   1 Draw the outline of an island on a large piece of paper (at least 30
                        cm × 40 cm), with a key to the picture symbols at the bottom (see
                        below). Do not put any symbols on the island itself at this stage.

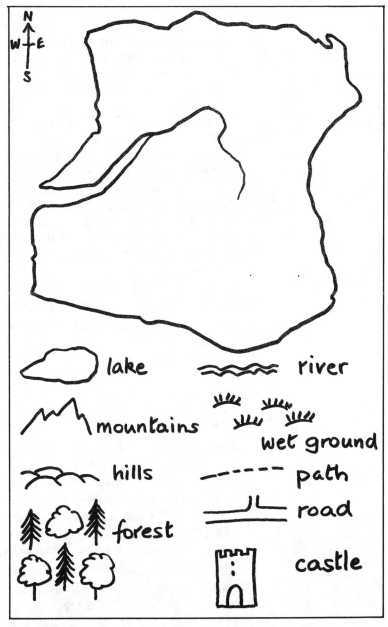

2 On a second large piece of paper write sentences like these (adapting for your class):

> *This is our island.*
> *Its name is ...*
> *These are the rivers.*
> *This one is ...*
> *That one is ...*
> *These are the people in the castle.*
> *We live in this hut/cave.*
> *This is our food. We find nuts here, fruit here, rabbits here, and fish here.*

3 Have ready the following:
   - a large sheet of paper and pencils for each group of three or four children (about 30 cm × 40 cm)
   - about six smaller sheets of paper for each group (about 20 cm × 30 cm)
   - about ten small cards (about 5 cm × 10 cm).

IN CLASS

1 Tell the children to relax and listen. Say something like:

> You are all on a plane. Suddenly the pilot says, 'There is something wrong'. And slowly the plane comes down on to the sea. Everybody gets into a lifeboat. All of you are safe and you are in different lifeboats. The wind blows you across the sea. Then you see some islands. Your boat comes to one of these small islands. There are some mountains on it and lots of trees. The other boats go to different islands.

Discuss this situation with the children to establish their vision of it and their feelings and ideas about it.

2 Make groups of three or four children per lifeboat. Tell them to begin by drawing the outline of their island; it must fill the top three-quarters of the paper. The outline must include one or two rivers. Show them your example.

Now ask the children to copy, at the bottom of their paper, the symbols: *lake, mountains, hills, forest, river, wet ground, path, road, castle.*

You might like to show the children a real map with pictographic symbols on it.

3 Discuss with each group how many of each feature they want to put on their island. For example, you might say:

You: *How many mountains are there on your island?*
Child: *Three.*
You: *Good. Draw three mountains on your island.*

Alternatively, tell each group how many features to draw:

There are three mountains. Draw them.
There are two rivers. Draw them.

4 Ask the children to fill in more details, for example:

Where do you arrive on the island? Draw an X.
Draw where you live. Write 'cave' or 'hut'.
Draw where you find food. Write 'fruit', 'rabbit', 'nuts', 'fish'.
Draw a man or a woman in or near the castle.
Write a name for your island, river, lake, mountains.

5 Display the islands on the wall.

Pair children from different groups to show their islands to each other. They should use the sentences on your poster to help them.

6 On a smaller piece of paper the children should draw pictures of:
   - their hut or cave
   - a plan showing where things are in the hut or cave
   - the food they find
   - the people in the castle
   - some dangerous animals

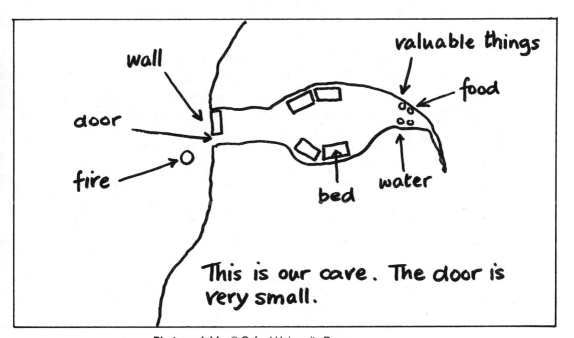

Photocopiable © Oxford University Press

They should write whatever they can about these drawings, using their dictionaries and you to help them, as necessary.

7 Help the children to make 'problem cards' and 'good fortune' cards, which they can pick up and incorporate during their adventurous tour. For example:

Some people chase you.
A snake bites you.
You fall in a river.
You are lost in a forest.

You fall and break your leg.
Some people tie you to a tree.
You find some treasure.
You find a lot of food and drink.
You find a telephone.

8   Now the children should plan, discuss, and draw the route they take around the island on their map. At about ten points on their route they should write a number to represent an incident or adventure which took place there.

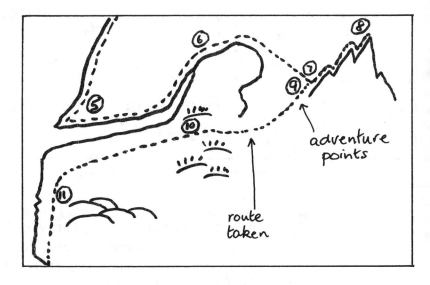

For each number they should write at least one sentence on a separate sheet of paper which will be the basis of a journal. This journal should only be a draft—when the whole adventure is over they can make a final version.

9 Make sure that each child in the group has a copy of his or her group's draft journal and that they can read it and understand it.

10 Pair off the children with children in other groups. Each child says what happened to them on their adventurous tour of the island (pointing at the numbers).

11 The children make new, more elaborate final drafts of their journals.

FOLLOW-UP   The maps may be used for further adventures, stories, or board games.

Examples
– Groups of children can visit each others' islands.
– The children can invent rules and laws for their island, and work out daily routines.
– They can put letters into bottles and throw them into the sea.

5.10 Guess the mime story

LEVEL   **Pre-intermediate**

LANGUAGE   **Fluency in all four skills with an emphasis on writing**

TIME   **30–40 minutes**

IN CLASS   1 Put the children into groups of four. Tell them to invent a story which they can mime so clearly that other groups will know what their story is. The mime should show emotions such as happiness, anger, and sadness, and must last no longer than two minutes. The groups rehearse their mimes.

2 Each group writes five key sentences from their story. (They must not write the story first and then try to mime it, because in that way they will not think in terms of mime.)

3 They perform their mime twice for another group of children, who try to guess what the story is.

4 They might now want to revise their mime if it is not clear.

5 If they have changed their mime, they rewrite their story sentences.

6 They mime for another group. Each group tries to guess the other's story and writes down five key sentences from it.

7 The groups compare the two sets of sentences. If the other group gets the general idea of the story, the performing group can feel pleased!

5.11 Music, questions, and a film story

LEVEL

Elementary to pre-intermediate

LANGUAGE

Fluency in all four skills

TIME

30–40 minutes

PREPARATION

Select three pieces of music, each about two or three minutes long. Make sure they are of very different kinds.

IN CLASS

1 Play the first piece of music as the children come into the class. Turn it down (but not off). Tell the children that they are going to invent their own opening for a film. Tell them that the film will be in their heads.

2 Tell the children to close their eyes. They should listen to the music, imagine a place, look at it, listen to it, feel it, and smell it.

3 After two or three minutes tell the children to open their eyes and to write down lots of words and short phrases describing the place they saw in their imagination. Give them two or three minutes to do this.

   If children ask for help, you can write words and phrases on the board and say that anyone can borrow anything written there.

4 Tell the children to listen to the next piece of music with their eyes closed, and to imagine a person or people in their place. What do they look like? What are they doing? Who are they?

5 After two or three minutes tell the children to open their eyes and to write down lots of words and short phrases describing the people they saw in their imaginations.

6 In pairs, the children tell each other about their ideas from listening to the music.

7 Play one more piece of music and now ask the children to look at the people in their imagination again, if they can, and see what the people are doing and where they are. They write these down.

8 The children now form new pairs and try to tell each other their film story opening, based on the notes they have made.

9 Repeat Step 8 with new pairs. The point of this work in pairs is to give the children the opportunity to build up the idea of their story orally before they attempt to do it in writing.

10 The children write up their story, preferably in a form which will allow them to publish it as a book (see Chapter 8).

FOLLOW-UP

The children work in groups listening to each other's stories and select one to dramatize as a group. If you have the facilities, they can make a video.

6 Sorting and sequencing

In this family of activities the children have a lot of 'bits of information' in no particular sequence. They must use some or all of the information to make their story.

The bits of information may come from you and/or from the children and can be perceived through any of the five senses:

Seeing

pictures (abstract, magazine, children's own pictures, pictures on the board, maps, pictographs, etc.)

written texts (sentences, letters, newspaper articles or headlines, bus tickets, notes, postcards)

objects (bag, jacket, spectacles, box)

actions (mime, drama, or real happenings in the school)

Hearing

spoken texts heard on tape (bits of conversation overheard, an interview with someone)

sounds (chance sounds from outside the classroom, taped sounds)

Feeling and smelling

objects (flowers, food, books, cloth, branches, pets, boxes, keys)

Tasting

food and drink

6.1 A near-beginners' story

LEVEL

Near-beginners and above

LANGUAGE

Fluency in listening and speaking

TIME

20–30 minutes

PREPARATION

Find three or four magazine pictures large enough for the class to see. They should also be quite interesting and the sort of pictures which the children might know the English words for, for example: *man, house, dog, three, red.*

IN CLASS

1 Show the class the magazine pictures. You can walk around to give individual children a closer look. Tell the class that you are going to help them to make a story.

2 Ask the children to call out any words or phrases they can connect with the picture. Write these on the board, whatever they are. Group the words for each picture you show. Put up the pictures on the board with the words.

3 Remind the children that you are going to tell their story. Ask them to tell you any more words they can think of related to the pictures and to a possible story.

4 Use the children's mother tongue to help them to create a story based on the pictures and words they have in English. Retell the story to them in English, pointing to the pictures and the words.

FOLLOW-UP

Type or write out the children's story at home, making use of as many of their words and phrases as possible. Make a big book of it if possible (see 8.4). Take the story to the class and read it to them. In this way you will be able to read the story with the class very easily—and it will be their book!

6.2 Story in a tin

LEVEL

Elementary and above

LANGUAGE

Fluency in all four skills

TIME

20–30 minutes

MATERIALS

A clean tin or a small box, a slip of paper or thin card for each child (you can get these free from stationers or printers where they cut card).

IN CLASS

1 Each child writes a sentence on a slip of paper or card and drops it into your tin. You do the same.

2 Take a slip of paper from the tin. Read out the sentence and then begin a story, making use of all or part of the sentence.

3 The children each take a sentence from the tin. They take it in turns to continue the story. As soon as they think their sentence can follow the previous one they put up their hands to go next. If you wish, they can stand in line holding their sentences.

VARIATION 1

1 Each child has five cards and writes a word or phrase on each card. Each child puts his or her cards into an envelope.

2 The children work in groups of three or four to arrange the cards into a sequence and to make a story incorporating them all.

VARIATION 2

With lower-proficiency children you can play a bigger role, for example, by guiding and boosting the story with questions (see 2.6, 'Someone in a hole'). You can also make it easier by providing a theme.

6.3 Sort and sequence the sentences

The children put texts together in any sequence they wish in order to make their own story.

LEVEL

Elementary and above

LANGUAGE

Fluency with emphasis on reading and writing

TIME

30–40 minutes

MATERIALS

Ten long strips of paper for each pair of children (about 5 cm × 30 cm), and if possible much longer strips for yourself (at least 50 cm × 5 cm); large pieces of paper.

IN CLASS

1 Ask the class to call out up to ten sentences in English. Write them on the board. The sentences can be totally arbitrary or you can ask the children to think of sentences which might be useful in making a story. For example:

Good morning!   *The boy is running.*
Where is Katy?   *I can hear a strange noise.*

2 The children copy the sentences onto their strips of paper.

3 Tell the children to arrange the strips so that they begin to make a story. Show them how to do this by sticking strips on the board in a sequence. Let them hear you trying to work out a story. Demonstrate how it may be necessary to add extra material.

4 When the children are sure they can tell a story based on their sequence they should stick their strips onto a big piece of paper. They can then join another pair who have finished and exchange stories.

VARIATION 1

Instead of the children inventing the sentences you can prepare them yourself. Give each group the same sentences so that it is more interesting for them to compare their stories.

VARIATION 2

1 You or the children can cut up a newspaper or magazine and stick down single words or short texts. Photocopy them and give each pair of children a sheet.

2 The children try to refer to or to include all the texts in their story.

VARIATION 3

Each child invents a sentence and writes it down on a small piece of paper or card. All the children then walk about and read their sentences to each other. After some minutes, tell the children to get into groups of five or six and to make a story based on the sentences of the children in their group.

VARIATION 4

Show the children a picture and ask them to call out words and phrases they associate with it. Try to make up a story in three minutes with their words. Now challenge the children to invent another story in three minutes based on the same words.

COMMENTS

Trying to sequence jumbled words and sentences in order to reconstruct a story is a well-known and useful activity. This activity is not quite that—there is no right or wrong sequence.

6.4 Massive graffiti mural story

LEVEL

Elementary and above

LANGUAGE

Reading and writing fluency and accuracy

TIME

30 minutes +

MATERIALS

A huge piece of paper, the bigger the better.

IN CLASS

1 Show the children the big piece of paper you have put on the wall and tell them that you want them to enjoy themselves. They can draw, stick magazine pictures, or write anything on the paper providing it is in English. (If you want to have some control over it then you can insist on seeing everything before it is put on the paper.) Everything must have the originator's name on it.

2 In groups or as a whole class, the children invent and then write a story which includes a reference to every single drawing or text on the giant graffiti mural.

3 Display the stories alongside the mural.

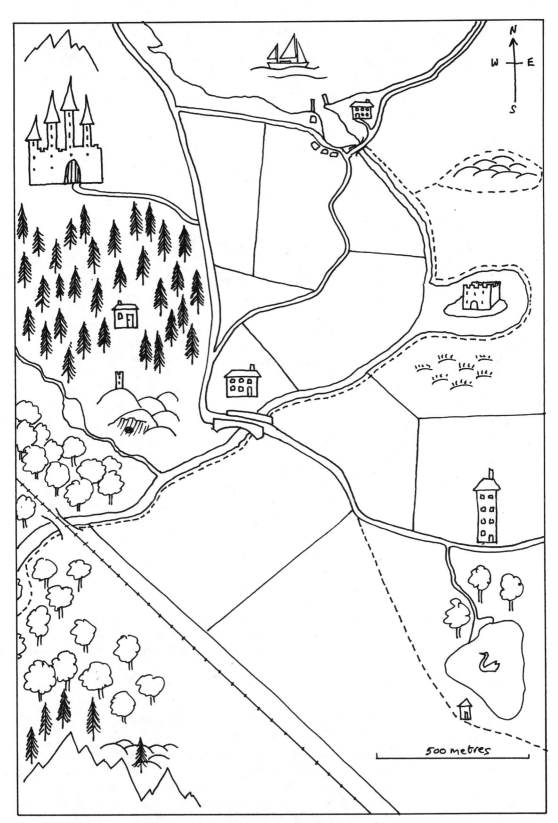

VARIATION 1

Make a massive bird's eye view map showing roads, railways, paths, streams, rivers, bridges, woods, cliffs, caves, houses, factories, schools, shops, castles, airports, etc. The children can wander around the map and invent stories and live out dramas.

Help the children to keep each thing they draw to some kind of common scale.

VARIATION 2

If you want to help the children to write the story you can insist that they put words and phrases even on the pictures (you must check these before they are put on the mural). In this way the children have to combine words and phrases more than originate them.

6.5 Thank you for your letter

In this activity the children pretend to be characters from well-known stories and write letters to each other.

LEVEL

Pre-intermediate

LANGUAGE

Letter-writing, fluency in all four skills

TIME

30–40 minutes

MATERIALS

As many small cards (approximately 5 cm × 10 cm) as there are children in the class (or half that number if you want them to work in pairs).

PREPARATION

Jot down all the stories you think the children know. You can include any type of story: traditional stories and fables from anywhere in the world, modern children's stories, stories in films or television, rhymes and songs, etc. Check that you know the main storyline of each.

IN CLASS

1 Brainstorm on the board all the names of story characters you and the class can think of. If you are not sure of the English name use the name in the children's mother tongue. Try to make sure that you finish up with as many different names as there are children in the class. Don't forget to include minor characters. (If you want the children to work in pairs then you will only need half the number of characters.)

Ask for two or three 'secretaries' to copy the names on to small pieces of card as you continue with Step 2. They should put all the names into a box.

2 Now you must help the children to see how these characters from so many different stories could relate to each other. Ask for someone to volunteer to be one of the characters. Pretend to be another character yourself. Introduce yourself. Begin a dialogue with the child who has volunteered to be another character. For example:

You: (as the Mother Bear in 'Goldilocks and The Three
        Bears') *Hello! I'm Mother Bear! Who are you?*
Child: (as the hunter in 'Little Red Riding Hood') *Hello! I'm
        the hunter.*
You: *Where is that girl—what's her name?*
Child: *Little Red Riding Hood.*
You: *Where is she?*
Child: *She's at home.*

3 Ask the children to take a name at random from the box. That
  is going to be their name for this activity. Pairs just take one
  name. As they take their name you can ask them who they are
  and which story they come from.

4 They should now go back to their places and write down their
  names and one or two sentences about themselves on the back
  of their card (see Preparation).

Examples

I am a king. I'm not happy.
I am a lion. I live in a cave. I want to eat the little Indian boy.

5 The children put all the name cards back in the box and take
  another name. (Pairs continue to act like one person.)

6 The children now write a letter to the character on the card
  they have taken from the box. They write as if they are their
  first character.

Example

> Dear Wolf
> I am sorry you are in hospital.
> And I am sorry you ate Little
> Red Riding Hood and then
> lost her.
> I wanted to eat a little Indian
> boy but he ran away. So I do
> understand your problem!
> Come to my cave and I will
> give you a good dinner!
> Good luck! Get better soon!
> Love
>   Lion

7 Lion now delivers his letter to Wolf. Wolf writes a reply to Lion.

8 Collect the letters and display them together.

9 Make them into a class book.

VARIATION 1

With higher-proficiency groups, discuss with the children the variety of letters they might send: suggesting, complaining, inviting, apologizing, and so on.

VARIATION 2

Help even lower-proficiency children to write a simple letter, for example:

Dear Mr Wolf,
You are very bad. You eat children. Please eat ice cream.
Yours, Goldilocks.

VARIATION 3

The children can write other types of text for their characters, for example, diary entries or shopping lists.

Acknowledgements

I got this idea from *The Jolly Postman* by Janet and Allan Ahlberg, which has become a classic book for children in recent years. It is made almost entirely of actual envelopes each containing a letter from a great range of well-known characters from traditional stories: The Three Bears, Goldilocks, The Wicked Witch, The Giant, Cinderella, B. B. Wolf, etc.

6.6 A story of gestures

LEVEL

Pre-intermediate

LANGUAGE

Fluency in all the skills

TIME

Steps 1 to 4: 30 minutes, Steps 5 and 6: 30 minutes, Step 7: 40–50 minutes.

PREPARATION

1 Choose up to ten gestures you think your children can already describe in English and one or two more you think they could learn easily. Write your selection on a large piece of paper or an overhead projector transparency. For example:

Nod your head  You are saying 'Yes'.

Shake your head.  You are saying 'No'.

Raise your right hand and beckon with your forefinger. You are saying 'Come here'.

Hold up one hand with the palm away from you. 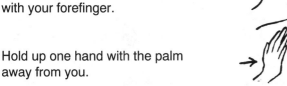 You are saying 'Stop'.

Tap the side of your head. You are saying that someone is stupid or crazy.

Look angry/happy/unhappy/ surprised/disgusted. You are angry, etc.

Wave your forefinger from side to side.  You are saying 'No, don't do that'.

Wave one hand from side to side with your palm away from you. You are saying 'Goodbye'.

Put your hands on your waist and tap your foot. You are saying you are impatient.

Sweep your hand and arm towards you and past you. You are saying 'Come in'.

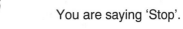

2 Practise your gestures. Make them clear, slow, and exaggerated.

IN CLASS

1 Mime your gestures in random order. Ask the children to say what you are miming.

2 Ask volunteers to mime particular gestures and ask the class to guess what they are doing. Help the children to mime clearly, slowly, and with exaggeration.

3 Divide the class into groups of three or four. Each group must select five of the gestures and build up a story based on them. They should rehearse their story until they have got it right.

4 Each group then mimes their story to the class as a whole. The class try to guess what the story was about and list the five gestures the story was based on.

FOLLOW-UP 1

Each group mimes their story again, but this time one child in the group narrates the story.

FOLLOW-UP 2

Each group writes and illustrates their story, making a book of five pages plus one cover (see Chapter 8).

6.7 Story maze

The children 'write their way' across a maze of pictures and texts.

LEVEL

Elementary and above

LANGUAGE

Fluency in all four skills with a focus on writing

TIME

30–40 minutes

PREPARATION

If you would like to keep the maze then you will need a large piece of paper plus a variety of broad colour markers.

IN CLASS

1 Ask for volunteer children to draw pictures or write phrases or sentences on the board or on a large piece of paper in exactly ten seconds. Two or three children can draw at the same time. When they have finished, draw circles round the pictures or texts and then join them together.

2 Show the children how they can create a story linking each one of the pictures or texts. Here are the opening sentences of two stories at different proficiency levels, based on the maze below:

Elementary

It is 12 o'clock. It is the middle of the night. Jim drives his car. There is a river. There is a man in the river. The man shouts. Jim hears the man ...

Pre-intermediate
It was a dark and windy night. Jim Beaver was driving his car It was difficult; the road turned to the left and to the right ...

3 The children, working in pairs, now plan their own way through the maze. They should work out their story orally and should make sure that each one of them can tell the story. (As in all of these activities they must plan their story according to the English they have.)

4 Ask one or two pairs to volunteer to stand by the board and tell their story to the whole class. As they tell the story the rest of the class (and you) try to imagine which way they are going through the maze.

5 The children now make new pairs. Each child tells the story he or she created. Their partner must decide which way the other child went. (This step can be repeated several times so that each child tells his or her story several times.)

FOLLOW-UP   The children make a copy of the maze and write their story to make a book.

6.8 Who, what, where

LEVEL   Elementary and above

LANGUAGE   Oral fluency

TIME   20–30 minutes

MATERIALS   An object, a picture of a person, and a place for each child.

IN CLASS
1 Give each child:
   – a photograph of a person
   – a postcard or picture of a place
   – a real object (e.g. a key, a cup, a coin)
2 The children arrange their objects in an order and then create a story about them. They tell the story to several other children.

7 Starting with one thing

In this family of activities the children start off with a single stimulus of some kind. It might be a beautiful evocative picture, an ambiguous picture, a drawing by the child, a piece of music, a sentence, a word, an object, a memory, a person, a puppet, a teddy bear, or a strange-shaped but empty book.

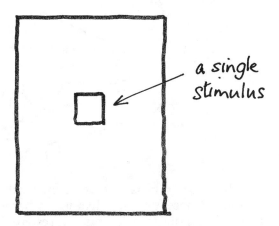

a single stimulus

The advantage of starting with one thing is that the child can really concentrate on it and search out its special details and its special associations for him or her.

The technique of bubbling and clustering, discussed in Chapter 3, is particularly useful for stirring up associations, memories, connections, and relevant words and phrases related to the initial stimulus.

7.1 Funny fellow

The children draw an imaginary picture, annotate it, and write a story about it.

LEVEL	**Beginners and above**
LANGUAGE	**Written fluency**
TIME	**20 minutes**
MATERIALS	A large piece of paper for the class 'funny fellow'; a smaller piece of paper for each child (about 20 cm × 30 cm).

IN CLASS

1 Draw an imaginary picture on the board or on a large piece of paper. Here is an example (not annotated) by Martina Hall from Klagenfurt in Austria.

2 Ask the children to say whatever they can about it, for example, where it is and when it is, what it is doing, where it is going. Write their words and phrases around the picture.

3 Say, *Oh, dear! Oh, dear! What's wrong?* Encourage the children to think of things which might go wrong for the 'funny fellow' you have drawn.

4 Ask the children to each draw their own funny fellow, to write a lot of words and phrases around it, and then to invent a short story about it.

FOLLOW-UP

Make a class book of funny fellows.

VARIATION

You can ask the children to make an annotated drawing on another theme:

– an early memory
– a strange machine
– a horrible thing.

7.2 A special picture

LEVEL

Elementary and above

LANGUAGE

Written fluency

TIME

30 minutes

MATERIALS	Find a beautiful picture, big enough for the whole class to see. There should be a feeling of a place, people, and a dramatic happening in the picture.

IN CLASS

1 Begin by showing the picture to the children and getting them to call out lots of words and phrases they associate with it. Write these on the board.
2 Ask the children what they can see, hear, feel, smell, and taste in the picture.
3 Ask the children what the people in the picture (if there are any) are thinking, feeling, and saying.
4 Ask the children where they would like to be in the picture. What are they doing, thinking, feeling, and saying?
5 Write on the board:

   Beginning   Action   End

   Ask the children to write a three-part story with the picture as the source of their ideas.

FOLLOW-UP

Make a class book with a copy of the picture or the picture itself as the front page.

7.3 Ambiguous pictures

LEVEL

Beginners and above

LANGUAGE

Fluency in speaking and writing

TIME

20–30 minutes

IN CLASS

1 Draw a rectangle on the board. Then, very slowly, draw a line across the rectangle, about one-third of the way from the bottom.

2 Ask what the children can see in the picture. They may say something like: *It's a line. That's the sky. It's a wall. That's a field. It's the sea. It's a road.*

3 Draw a box-like rectangle on the line. Ask what it is. Possible answers: *It's a box. It's a hole. It's a door. It's a window. It's a car.*

4 Draw a stick person on the line near the box. Ask who he or she is and what he or she is doing/is going to do/has done. Possible answers: *It's a man/woman/boy/girl. He's looking at the box. He's a giant and that's a house. He's going into the house.*

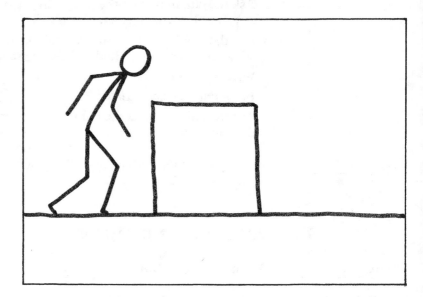

5 The children now work in pairs, draw the ambiguous picture, and invent a story to say what happens.

FOLLOW-UP 1

The children devise their own ambiguous pictures and exchange them with other children to invent stories about.

FOLLOW-UP 2

They can write the stories down and maybe make books.

COMMENTS

It is important to brainstorm a lot of ideas in order to open the imagination of all the children. It is also helpful to put a lot of the words and phrases on the board and leave them there.

7.4 Eyes closed

LEVEL

Elementary and above

LANGUAGE

Fluency in all the skills with an emphasis on listening

TIME

Steps 1 to 4: 20 minutes, plus 20 minutes to write the first draft of the story

MATERIALS

A big bunch of keys, preferably old keys.

IN CLASS

1 Show the keys to the children. Let them hear them as well as see them. You do not need to say very much at this stage—let the children's imagination begin to work.

2 Tell them that you are going to ask them to close their eyes and then ask them some questions. They must answer in their own minds and not speak their answers.

Ask the children to close their eyes and to make themselves comfortable.

3 Begin your description and ask your questions, for example:

> You are looking at a door. Is it a big door or a little door? Is it an old door or a new door? Is it painted or is it wooden? Is the door in a wall? Of a house or something else? Is the wall made of stone, or brick, or is it painted? Look closely at it. What can you see?
> You are holding the key. Put the key in the lock of the door. Turn it. Open the door. Go through the door. Stop. What can you see? What can you hear? What can you smell? What does it feel like? Do you like it? Stay for a moment, look, listen, and feel.
> Now come back. Close the door again. Open your eyes when you are ready.

4 Ask the children to tell their neighbours what they saw and felt.

5 Tell them to write a short story which describes going through the door and then what happened next.

VARIATION

Here is another example making use of what is probably within the scope of most children who are in their second year of English:

> Close your eyes. You are in a park. It is a lovely day. The sun is shining. Some children are playing with a ball. You don't want to play with the children. You walk across the grass. You come to some trees. There are no people, no grown-ups, no children. But you see a big dog. It is a beautiful dog. The dog smiles at you and wags its tail. You are not frightened of the dog. You follow the dog. The grass is long and you cannot hear your feet. The wind is blowing but you can't hear the wind. Then you hear music. The music is quiet and slow. You walk slowly and you look to the left and to the right. But you follow the dog. The dog goes behind a big tree. You can't see the dog. You go around the tree—what can you see? What can you hear? What happens?

COMMENTS

1 You can launch the children into their deep imagination again and again. Each time you do it you oil the door of their imagination and make it familiar to them. In this example a bunch of keys is used but this is not essential. You can use other stimuli, or help the children to look at their inner images just by speaking.

2 Most of the language you use should be known to them so that they are not reminded of the limitations of their language and then dragged spluttering to the surface.

8 Making books

There are two main ways of making stories and books, and we need them both.

1 **Creating the story then the book:** A conventional book helps the children to make their stories more widely available and more professional looking.

2 **Creating the book then the story:** Creatively and unconventionally designed books are not just used to put stories in, but inspire the stories themselves by their special character.

Conventional books

Conventional books are for stories that are already created by the child. They represent the end of the process and give the child a reason for wanting to do well, to write a good story, and to write accurately in English. The book can be taken home, read in other classes, put in the school library, exhibited in a showcase, sent to twin schools in other countries, and so on. This sense of audience is wonderfully motivating for children.

How to make conventional books

The **zigzag** book is one of the most useful types of book: it is easy and fast to make; it can be as long or short as necessary; it can be read like a normal book, or displayed open on a table or wall. If several children are contributing to the book they should work on separate pages which are then glued into the zigzag book.

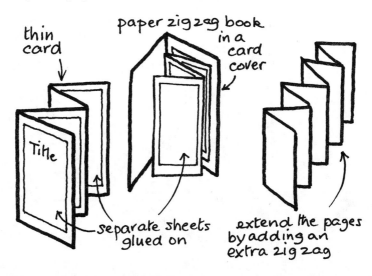

thin card

paper zigzag book in a card cover

Title

separate sheets glued on

extend the pages by adding an extra zigzag

The **folded sheet book** is easy to do but is of a fixed length and the children must work on separate sheets and stick them into the book if they are working as a group.

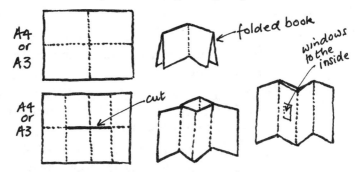

The **centre-stapled book** is the design used by most publishers for slim books. The advantages are that it is easy and fast to do if you have a long arm stapler, and that it opens flat. If you do not have a long-arm stapler a normal stapler can be used, opened wide with an eraser underneath. The pages can also be sewn together.

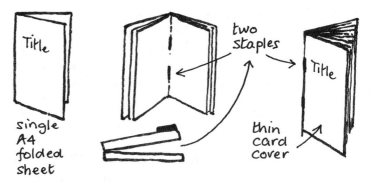

The **side-stapled book** does not open flat and this is a disadvantage, but it allows a lot of separate pages to be put together. The staples and the spine do not look good but they can be covered with plastic binding or masking tape.

The **tied book** can be opened flat if the thread (string, tape, wool) is loose enough, but then the book has a floppy feel about it. It is a quick way of putting together any number of pages. Tied tightly the book has a more professional 'feel' but it cannot be opened flat.

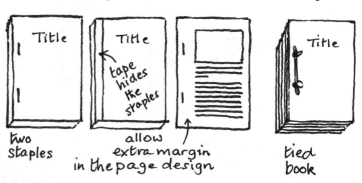

Another easy way to make 'books' of your children's work is simply to put them in a binder (they can design a picture for the cover).

Note that printers usually have off-cuts—strips of paper and card which have been cut off large pieces of paper. They will normally give these to you for nothing.

Tips on designing

It is important for children to learn that the professional presentation of ideas is an important part of successful communication. You might like to make a collection of published picture books and study with the children how they have been designed.

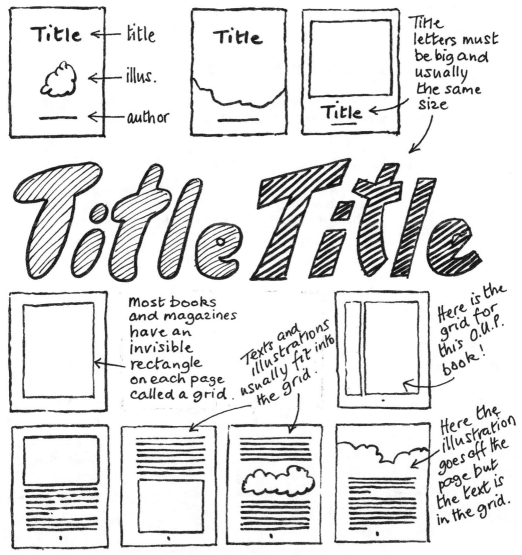

Title ← title
illus. ←
author ←

Title

Title

Title ←

Title letters must be big and usually the same size

Title Title

Most books and magazines have an invisible rectangle on each page called a grid.

Texts and illustrations usually fit into the grid.

Here is the grid for this O.U.P. book!

Here the illustration goes off the page but the text is in the grid.

Word processors or handwriting?

Word processors are increasingly available in schools and more and more children are becoming computer-literate. Word processors allow us fiddle around with alternative sentences, words, word order, and punctuation. We can print drafts and go away and read them and correct them. Most programs will allow us to think about the typeface we use, and the appearance of the final copy. We are all ready for publishing!

Word processors give children a sense of responsibility for what they do, so if they are available I recommend that you let the children try writing with them.

However, do not make children think that handwriting is 'not as good' as word-processing. Learning to write neatly is a worthwhile aim in itself. It is all the more important to practise handwriting if the native language has a different script from English.

Unconventional books

Unconventional books are made before the story is created and then they inspire and guide the stories by their design.

How to make unconventional books

A **flap** can represent an object, for example, a door or a cushion. When it is opened or lifted something is revealed! A well-known flap book is *Where's Spot?* by Eric Hill (see 2.9).

Flaps can open sideways, upwards, or downwards. The paper of the flap should be the same weight as the page rather than heavier. The sticky tape for the hinge must be exactly the same length and no longer than the part to be hinged, or it will not open.

Is he under the cushion?

flap book

Is he behind the curtain?

flap book

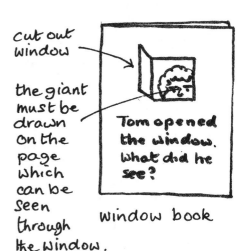

cut out window

the giant must be drawn on the page which can be seen through the window.

Tom opened the window. What did he see?

window book

letter book

Mobius Strip for everlasting stories.

←scroll book for old legends.

←flaps

multi flap book

In **window books** there are holes in the pages which allow you to see through to the page below. A well-known example of this is *The Very Hungry Caterpillar* by Eric Carle.

The hole can be completely cut out or cut as a flap which might be a window, door, or lid of a box.

Windows are not easy for children to cut because you need pointed scissors to get started, or you must fold the paper. Nevertheless, children love them and their imaginations are stimulated by them.

Encourage the children to use their imaginations and to think of several ideas. The children can then draw on the window, door, or lid to make it look like the object they have chosen. They should open their window, door, or lid and imagine what they can see underneath and draw it onto the page below. They then can turn the page over and complete the drawing. As they make their drawings they should begin to think of how the story might develop and the part that the window, door, or lid might play in the story.

A **pocket** can be stuck onto a page with a letter or object or person placed inside. The pocket can be left just as a paper pocket or might be drawn on so that it looks like an envelope and even have a flap. A well-known example of this idea is *The Jolly Postman* by Janet and Allan Ahlberg (full of envelopes and letters). This is an excellent idea for children because it combines two types of writing: the writing of the story and the writing of the letter. (See also 6.4, 'Thank you for your letter'.)

Pop-up books can be made quite easily by children, and give them great pleasure. Ideas for making 'beak books', 'boxes', and 'jump-up figures' are given in the activities below.

Shape books are not rectangular and their special shapes suggest various people places, and objects. These in turn suggest how the story in the book might develop.

8.1 Making a zigzag book step by step

LEVEL	**All**
LANGUAGE	**Any**
TIME	**30–40 minutes**
MATERIALS	One small sheet of paper per child, plus a few spare. Large pieces of thin coloured card or thick paper—one for every eight children. One knife or pair of big scissors for you to cut the card. Two or three glue sticks. Pens, pencils, erasers, etc. for each child.
PREPARATION	1 Cut the card into long strips. The strips must be a little taller than the paper you are going to stick on them.
	2 Fold the strips into sections which are a little wider than the sheets of paper you are going to stick on them (at least 1 cm on each side).

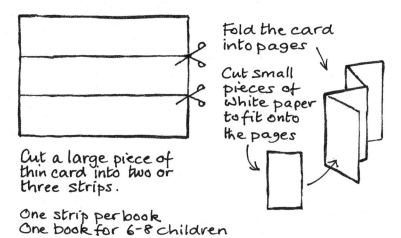

Fold the card into pages

Cut small pieces of white paper to fit onto the pages

Cut a large piece of thin card into two or three strips.

One strip per book
One book for 6–8 children

3 Place the classroom tables together for groups of about six to eight children.

Write on the board what should go on each page

Cover
1 mountain / Harry / 90 year old / rain
2 crocodile snake / 40 metres long / cave
3 Harry into cave / snow / cave light
4 Crocodile + Harry / secret passage
5 gold / treasure
6 to town / crocodile / Harry kisses it
7 Harry young! / crocodile young woman / marry

IN CLASS

1 Invent the story first, orally or in writing. Many of the activities given in this book lead to stories which you can put into book form.

2 Show the children the folded strips of card and the small sheets of paper. Show them how many pages there will be (most books have seven plus a front cover). Remember you can count the pages round the back of the zigzag book!

3 Divide the story into the same number of parts as you have pages available. For example, if you have a cover and seven pages, divide your story into seven parts. You can write a list of parts on the board.

4 Put the children into groups. It is a good idea to have fewer children than there are pages so that a child who finishes first can do another page (one child designs the cover).

5 The groups decide which child does which page.

6 Give each child a sheet of paper. As you do so, ask which page they are doing and get them to write the page number in the middle near the bottom.

7 The children design, write, and illustrate each page on the sheets of paper.

8 The children show you their page before they stick it into the book so that you can check their English.

COMMENTS

1 Instructions are given here for groupwork rather than individual work. The advantages are that each child only has one or two pages to write and illustrate, and that the children must co-operate in order to make sure that the texts do not overlap. You can write a list of parts for each page on the board.

2 For beginners you can write the actual text for the children to copy.

8.2 Making pop-up books

LEVEL

All

LANGUAGE

Writing fluency

TIME

60–80 minutes

MATERIALS

About four sheets of paper per child to practise on (about 20 cm × 30 cm). One larger piece of paper per child for their final book (about 30 cm × 40 cm). One pair of scissors for each pair of children.

PREPARATION

1 Make a photocopy of the worksheet 'How to make a beak book' for each child (see overleaf).

2 Most important! Practise making a beak book yourself before the lesson.

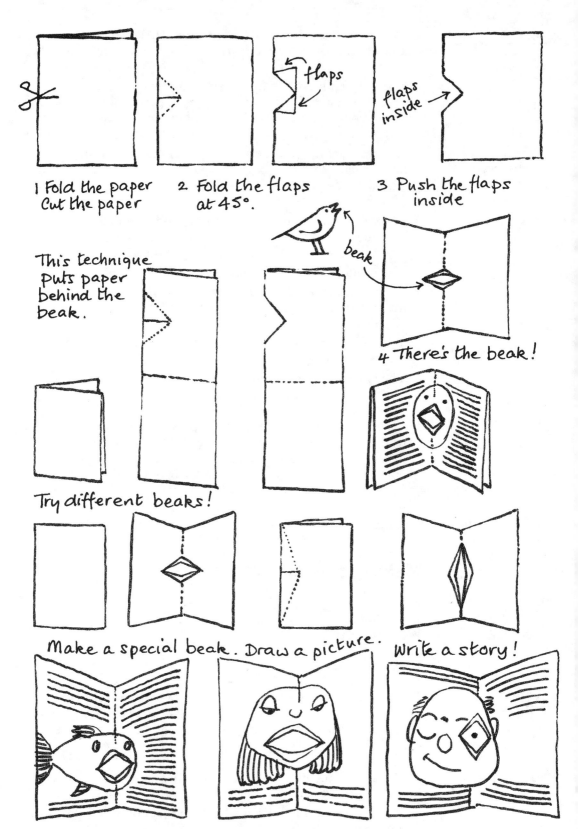

1 Fold the paper
   Cut the paper

2 Fold the flaps
   at 45°.

flaps

3 Push the flaps
   inside

flaps inside →

beak

This technique
puts paper
behind the
beak.

4 There's the beak!

Try different beaks!

Make a special beak. Draw a picture. Write a story!

IN CLASS

1 Show the children a beak book you have made.
2 Hand out the worksheets. Let the children look at them.
3 Demonstrate how to make a beak book, slowly. The children should watch you and follow their instruction sheet, but not do it themselves yet.
4 Give out the necessary materials and tell the children to make their own beak book following the instructions on the worksheet. If you want them to experiment with different beaks, give each child more than one piece of paper.
5 As the children experiment with different beaks ask them what they think theirs might be. Here are some possibilities but please be open to their more imaginative ideas and provide any words they need to know with your dictionary, if necessary.

   bird   fish   person   monkey   tiger   dog   rat   space creature

6 Ask the children to draw their creature or person on the paper with the 'beak' as part of their story. Tell them to leave space for the story!
7 Ask some of the children if they would like to show their drawing to the class. Focus the children's minds on how to make a story by asking them (and the class) to imagine something about the person or creature. You might like to write key words on the board.
8 Ask the children to draft their story in pencil.
9 As the children finish, ask them to show their drawings and to read their story to another child who has finished. They make corrections in the light of feedback (see the Introduction, pages 6–9).
10 When you and the children feel that their stories are satisfactory, ask them to do a neat version.

VARIATIONS

More beaks and mouths

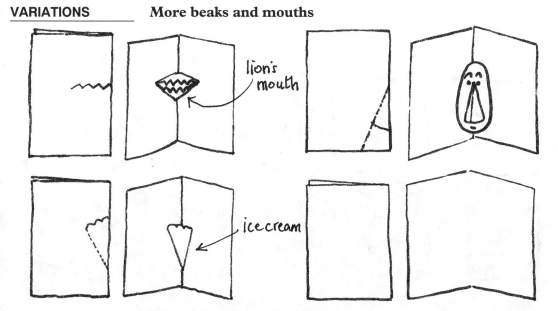

Jump out and up plus stick-on figure

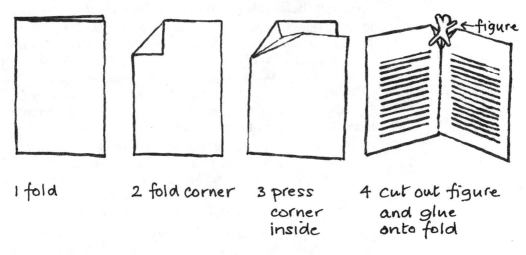

1 fold   2 fold corner   3 press   4 cut out figure
                                       corner   and glue
                                       inside   onto fold

Jump out and up cut-out figure

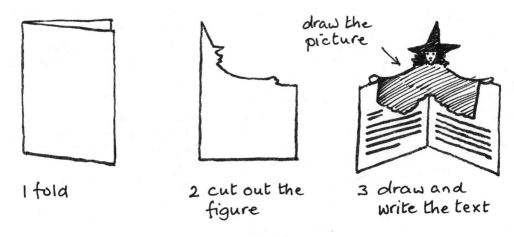

draw the
picture

1 fold   2 cut out the   3 draw and
                      figure   write the text

Boxes

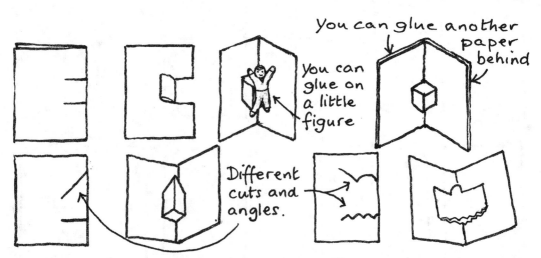

You can glue another
paper
behind

You can
glue on
a little
figure

Different
cuts and
angles.

8.3 Making shape books

LEVEL	**All**
LANGUAGE	**Written fluency leading to accuracy in the second draft**
TIME	**60–80 minutes**

PREPARATION

1 If the children are going to make the book then you will need scissors for them and large sheets of plain white (or coloured) paper (about 40 cm × 60 cm). Cut the paper in half lengthways.

2 Otherwise, you can do the cutting for them. Cut four sheets at the same time.

IN CLASS

1 Show the children a new strip of paper which has not been cut.

Tell them it is going to be a book. Tell them how amazing it is that the book does not exist yet but it is going to be born, right here, in front of them. And the story does not exist yet and that is going to be born here in the classroom as well.

2 Fold the strip of paper in half, and then in half again. Now open it and begin to cut the top edge in any way you please.

Now fold it into a book again and show the children the pages one by one. Ask them what they think the shapes look like. Here is an example with some words and phrases called out by children:

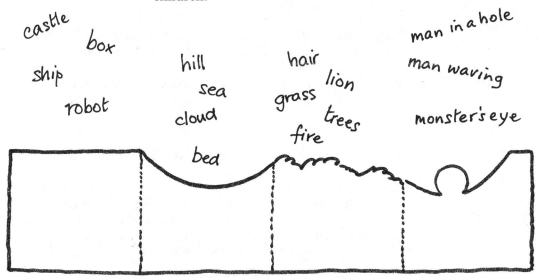

3 Give each child a piece of paper and a pair of scissors.

4 Tell the children to fold the paper into four parts. Then they should cut the top of the paper in any way they wish. They do not need their story ready before they begin, but they should begin to think of the story by looking at the shapes and thinking about them.

5 Walk around the class asking the children what they think their shapes might be. You will almost certainly need to give them some words they do not know. Do not hesitate to use a dictionary if you are unsure.

6 The children draw pictures to fit the shapes they have cut out.

7 The children draft their story in pencil and read it to at least two other children. This will tell them if their writing is clear.

8 They should then improve those parts which were difficult to read and understand. Finally they can write the words in pen.

cut out

↓

cut out

Add pictures to the shapes then text.

paper cut... letter put in...

FOLLOW-UP

As with all books, look for a wide audience. Exhibit the books in the school entrance hall, the head teacher's office, a local bookshop, and put them in the school library.

Use a good quality paper, for a final, published version, if possible. It encourages the children to do their best.

COMMENTS

If possible let the children make the book instead of making it for them. In the act of making it, the child can feel the story growing.

8.4 Making giant books and elf books

A giant book is a big book in which the text is so big that it can be read by children about three or four metres away from you. Giant books are useful for the early stages of reading when you sit together with all the children and read the text with them. The format of a giant book can also be used for other purposes, for example, picture collage.

LEVEL   **Beginners and elementary**

LANGUAGE   **Listening to stories; recognizing, writing, and adapting recurring patterns in a story**

TIME   **One hour of preparation plus 40–60 minutes in class**

MATERIALS   Sheets of paper for the pictures and sentences. These pieces of
paper should fit within the page size of the giant book. If you
want the children to make elf books (see Follow-up), have strips
of paper ready.

PREPARATION   1 Find stories which are very simple and depend almost entirely
on one sentence pattern which you feel is relevant to your
children. A well-known example is *Where's Spot?* by Eric Hill,
which practises 'Is he in/under the ...?'. For this pattern you
could also hide a toy in the classroom before the children
come in or give it to a child to put into his/her pocket.

2 Make a giant book before the lesson begins. One giant book is
big enough for about 20 children, working in pairs, one pair to
each page. If you have more children, prepare two giant books.

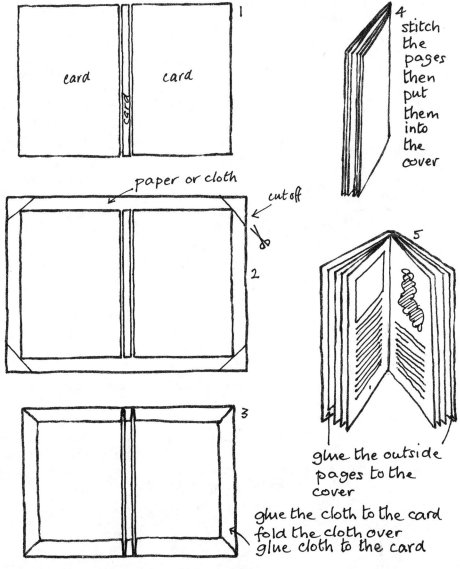

1 card   card   card

paper or cloth   cut off   2

3

4 stitch the pages then put them into the cover

5 glue the outside pages to the cover

glue the cloth to the card
fold the cloth over
glue cloth to the card

128   MAKING BOOKS

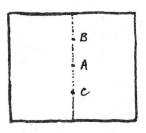

3a Push the needle through **A** from the inside of the book to the outside. Leave some thread sticking through inside the book.

b Push the needle through **B** from the outside to the inside.

c Push the needle through **C** from the inside to the outside.

d Push the needle through **A** from the outside to the inside.

e Cut the thread. Tie the two pieces of thread together, over the top of the long piece which goes from **B** to **C**.

IN CLASS

1 Tell the children a story which contains a clear, repeated sentence pattern.

Example

You: (looking frustrated) *Where's my little cat? Where is she?*

You: (indicating one of the children) *Anne! Is my little cat in your bag?*

Anne: (having a look) *No, she isn't. Ask Alan.* (You will have to ask her to tell you who to ask next.)

You: *Alan, is my little cat under your desk?*

Alan: (having a look) *No, she isn't. Ask Brian.*

You: *Oh, dear! Where is my little cat? Where is she?* (Nod at the child with the hidden toy.)

Eva: *Miaow!*

You: *Eva! Have you got my little cat? Yes? Oh, I'm so happy!*

Stop when you have gone through about ten locations.

2 With the children's help reconstruct the story and write the sentences on the board, related to the page numbers. Allow only one or two sentences for each page.

3 Now show them the giant book you want them to make into the story. Show the children the paper they will use for the pictures and for the text. Explain that the pictures must be very big and clear and the sentences very big and clear as well.

4 Put the children into pairs so that they work together to produce the illustration and the text for one page. One pair can do the title page and another can do the cover.

5 It is always a good idea to have one page which is not allocated. If a pair finishes very quickly and their work is acceptable then you can give them the extra page to do.

6 When the work is satisfactory you can stick it into the giant book.

FOLLOW-UP

Elf books

1 Help the children to make a story about one of their own pets. Use the same sentence patterns as you have written in the big book. They can change the pet, the places, and the prepositions if they want to.

2 To make it special, suggest that they make an elf book (a tiny book). The easiest way to do this is to fold a strip of paper to make a little zigzag book (see 8.1).

8.5 Making crazy books and stories

LEVEL	**All**
LANGUAGE	**Written fluency**
TIME	**60–80 minutes**
MATERIALS	Tools such as scissors, saws, metal cutters, glue, sticky tape, nails, wire, string pens, and paints.

Ask the children to bring whatever materials they can into the classroom and display them on tables—old paper, plastic, wood, metal, cloth, and similar objects.

IN CLASS

1 Announce that the class is going to make crazy books and when the children are finished they will vote for which is the craziest book.

2 Demonstrate to the children how they can become aware of the character of the materials. Show them a piece of paper—its smoothness, how it cuts, how holes can be made in it, how it can be folded or crumpled. Contrast it with other materials— the smoothness of plastic, the stiffness of wood, and so on.

3 Show the children the crazy book designs overleaf. If you like you can tell them they were made by children in Denmark.

4 Tell the children to work with a partner and choose some material, select part or parts of a story, and write it on, in, and under the material. They should be imaginative in their designs—a book can be anything which can be picked up and read.

5 As you go round to help the children, concentrate on the character of the material they have chosen. For example, the boys who made the 'cardboard plate and clear plastic cup book' began by writing across a cardboard plate. I showed pain on behalf of the plate: 'But it's round!' I said. When I came back they had written round the plate and been inspired to cut the spiral which fell into the clear plastic beaker.

FOLLOW-UP

These crazy books must be exhibited! The class who made these examples took them to a café next door and put them on the tables for the customers to look at.

Acknowledgements
The examples of crazy books were made by children aged thirteen to fourteen during a workshop in Helsingør in Denmark.

Cardboard Plate and Clear Plastic Cup Book

THE STAIRCASE PETER PAN AND GUY BRUSH HERE

white cardboard plate

clear plastic cup

You can read the story from the top.

Scrumple Book

Write your story then crumple it then ask people to read it. → They can re-crumple it behind their backs and then read a new piece.

Brick and Strip Book

were many rooms in the house the

You pull the story through the brick.

Cone and Mirror Book

look through the top of the cone.

cone

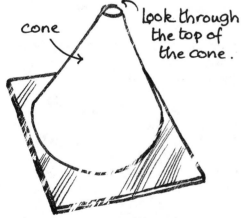

The story is written back to front on the paper. The paper is made into a cone.

You look through the top of the cone and read the story in the mirror.

A Two Clear Plastic Cup Book

The story is written on the inner cup.

Hold the outer cup and turn the inner cup and read the story.

Pete ran and Guy B were very sad becau both wan to be the king ran and ran thru rooms of the castle dark and cold but at last they

Further reading

Ahlberg, A. and **J. Ahlberg.** 1986. *The Jolly Postman.* London: Heinemann.

Barrs, K. 1994. *Music Works.* Twickenham: Belair Publications.

Barton, B. and **D. Booth.** 1990. *Stories in the classroom.* Markham, Ontario: Pembroke Publishers. A very useful book.

Barton, B. 1986. *Tell me Another: Storytelling and Reading Aloud at Home, at School and in the Community.* Markham, Ontario: Pembroke Publishers.

Baudains, R. and **M. Baudains.** 1990. *Alternatives.* Harlow: Longman.

Bettleheim, B. 1990. *The Uses of Enchantment: The Meaning and Importance of Fairy Tales.* Harmondsworth: Penguin. This is just one book in my list which concentrates on what fairy stories might be offering our children beneath the surface level of entertainment. An important book.

Carle, E. 1970. *The Very Hungry Caterpillar.* Harmondsworth: Penguin. A classic children's picture book, also available in bilingual versions.

Colwell, E. 1991 (new edn). *Storytelling.* Stroud, UK: Thimble Press. A useful book from a great storyteller.

Corbett, P. and **B. Moses.** 1991. *My Grandmother's Motorbike.* Oxford: Oxford University Press. A wonderful source of rich ideas.

Emblem, V. and **H. Schmitz.** 1991. *Learning through Story.* Leamington Spa: Scholastic Publications.

Fulford, J., M. Hutchings, A. Ross, and **H. Schmitz.** 1992. *Bright Ideas for Drama.* Leamington Spa: Scholastic Publications. Most of these ideas for drama are essentially story-making ideas for encouraging the children to get into a story frame of mind.

Gersie, A. 1992. *Earthtales.* London: Merlin Press. An excellent source of short stories of the creation myth kind for retelling. Also interesting and useful classroom activities though not primarily intended for children.

Gersie, A. and **N. King.** 1990. *Storymaking in Education and Therapy.* London: Jessica Kingsley. This is an extremely rich source of short, traditional stories from a variety of cultures accompanied by 'humanistic' activities. Not designed for learners of foreign language but of great value never the less.

Gibson, R., C. Childs, and **C. Caudron.** 1993. *The Usborne Book of Dressing Up.* London: Usborne. This book includes sections on face painting and making masks, costumes, and fancy dress. This publisher produces a wide selection of books for children, many of which are full of delightfully-presented practical ideas. Usborne books are widely available throughout the world.

Hill, E. 1983. *Where's Spot?*. Harmondsworth: Penguin. A classic children's book. Available in many languages.

Howe, A. and **J. Johnson.** 1992. *Common Bonds.* London: Hodder and Stoughton. A very useful book.

Jennings, C. 1991. *Children as Story-tellers.* Melbourne: Oxford University Press.

Johnson, K. 1981. *Impro.* London: Methuen. An inspired book on digging out creativity in all of us.

Johnson, P. 1991. *A Book of One's Own.* London: Hodder and Stoughton. Both of the books by this author listed here are rich in ideas for creative book making with many suggestions given for associated language development.

Johnson, P. 1992. *Pop-up Paper Engineering.* London: Falmer Press.

Maley, A. and **A. Duff.** 1978. *Drama Techniques in Language Learning.* Cambridge: Cambridge University Press.

Morgan, J. and **M. Rinvolucri.** 1983. *Once Upon a Time.* Cambridge: Cambridge University Press. This was the first book in the field of using stories in language teaching and it is excellent.

Moskowitz, G. 1978. *Caring and Sharing in the Foreign Language Class.* Rowley, Mass.: Newbury House.

Pellowski, A. 1987. *The Family Storytelling Handbook.* London: Macmillan.

Phillips, S. 1993. *Young Learners.* Oxford: Oxford University Press.

Ralston, M. V. 1993. *An Exchange Of Gifts.* Markham, Ontario: Pippin Teacher's Library. Half the book is useful further reading as well as some practical ideas for storytelling and story creation.

Rosen, B. 1988. *And None of it was Nonsense.* London: Mary Glasgow Publications. The author has done a lot of work with inner city teenagers.

Rosen, B. 1991. *Shapers and Polishers.* London: Mary Glasgow Publications. A rich resource.

Rosen, M. 1989. *Did I Hear You Write?* London: André Deutsch. A very good poet, writer, and storyteller who gets people to listen to themselves.

Scher, A. and **C. Verrall.** 1975. *100+ Ideas for Drama.* Oxford: Heinemann.

Wagner, B.J. 1979. *Dorothy Heathcote: Drama as a Living Medium.* Cheltenham: Stanley Thornes. This is a very thorough and helpful description of an inspired teacher's way of working.

Watts, I.N. 1992. *Making Stories.* Markham, Ontario: Pembroke Publishers. A very good book particularly for helping children to make stories themselves.

Wingate, J. 1989. *Fun with Pictures.* Bristol: The Friendly Press.

An excellent collection of practical ideas including some for story making.

Wingate, J. 1990. *How to Use Storytelling in Language Teaching.* Bristol: Primary House. This author is a constant source of creative ideas.

Wray, D. 1987. *Bright Ideas Writing.* Leamington Spa: Scholastic Publications. Lots of practical ideas including ideas for story and poetry writing.

Wright, A. 1994 (2nd edn). *1000+ Pictures for Teachers to Copy.* London: Longman. More than 1000 pictures of everyday objects, people, animals and situations for teachers to copy. Based on wide experience of teachers' needs.

Wright, A. 1990. *Pictures for Language Learning.* Cambridge: Cambridge University Press. Over 350 ways of using magazine pictures and simple drawings for storytelling and writing.

Wright, A. 1995. *Storytelling with Children.* Oxford: Oxford University Press.

Wright, A., D. Betteridge, and **M. Buckby.** 1984. *Games for Language Learning.* Cambridge: Cambridge University Press. A large collection of games and activities for language teaching, many of which are useful in presenting and practising language items before a story is told. There is also an ideas section for story-making and writing.

Wright, A. and **P. Ur.** 1992. *Five-minute activities.* Cambridge: Cambridge University Press. A resource book of short activities, including several 'story warmers'.

Wright, A. and **S. Haleem.** 1991. *Visual Materials for the Language Classroom.* Harlow: Longman. Practical ideas for using all the media in the classroom creatively including story-making and writing.

Other titles in the Resource Books for Teachers series

Beginners, by Peter Grundy—over 100 original, communicative activities for teaching both absolute and 'false' beginners, including those who do not know the Latin alphabet. (ISBN 0 19 437200 6)

CALL, by David Hardisty and Scott Windeatt—a bank of practical activities, based on communicative methodology, which make use of a variety of computer programs. (ISBN 0 19 437105 0)

Class Readers, by Jean Greenwood—practical advice and activities to develop extensive and intensive reading skills, listening activities, oral tasks, and perceptive skills. (ISBN 0 19 437103 4)

Classroom Dynamics, by Jill Hadfield—a practical book to help teachers maintain a good working relationship with their classes, and so promote effective learning. (ISBN 0 19 437096 8)

Conversation, by Rob Nolasco and Lois Arthur—more than 80 activities which develop students' ability to speak confidently and fluently. (ISBN 0 19 437096 8)

Cultural Awareness, by Barry Tomalin and Susan Stempleski— activities to challenge stereotypes, using cultural issues as a rich resource for language practice. (ISBN 0 19 437194 8)

Drama, by Charlyn Wessels—first-hand, practical advice on using drama to teach spoken communication skills and literature, and to make language learning more creative and enjoyable. (ISBN 0 19 437097 6)

Exam Classes, by Peter May—includes activities to help prepare for a wide variety of public examinations, including most of the main American and British exams such as TOEFL and the new UCLES exams. (ISBN 0 19 437208 1)

Grammar Dictation, by Ruth Wajnryb—also known as 'dictogloss', this technique improves students' understanding and use of grammar by reconstructing texts. (ISBN 0 19 437097 6)

Learner-based Teaching, by Colin Campbell and Hanna Kryszewska—over 70 language practice activities which unlock the wealth of knowledge that learners bring to the classroom. (ISBN 0 19 437163 8)

Letters, by Nicky Burbidge, Peta Gray, Sheila Levy, and Mario Rinvolucri—demonstrates the rich possibilities of letters for language and cultural study. Contains numerous photocopiables and a section on email. (ISBN 0 19 442149 X)

Literature, by Alan Maley and Alan Duff—an innovatory book on using literature for language practice. (ISBN 0 19 437094 1)

Music and Song, by Tim Murphey—shows teachers how 'tuning

in' to their students' musical tastes can increase motivation and tap a rich vein of resources. (ISBN 0 19 437055 0)

Newspapers, by Peter Grundy—creative and original ideas for making effective use of newspapers in lessons. (ISBN 0 19 437192 6)

Project Work, by Diana L. Fried-Booth—practical resources to bridge the gap between the classroom and the outside world. (ISBN 0 19 437092 5)

Pronunciation, by Clement Laroy—imaginative activities to build confidence and improve all aspects of pronunciation. (ISBN 0 19 437089 9)

Role Play, by Gillian Porter Ladousse—from highly controlled conversations to improvised drama, and from simple dialogues to complex scenarios. (ISBN 0 19 437095 X)

Self-Access, by Susan Sheerin—helps teachers with the practicalities of setting up and managing self-access study facilities. (ISBN 0 19 437099 2)

Storytelling with Children, by Andrew Wright—30 stories plus hundreds of exciting ideas for using any story to teach English to children aged 7 to 14. (ISBN 0 19 437202 2)

Translation, by Alan Duff—provides a wide variety of translation activities from many different subject areas. (ISBN 0 19 437104 2)

Very Young Learners, by Vanessa Reilly and Sheila M. Ward—advice and ideas for teaching children aged 3 to 6 years. Over 80 activities including games, songs, drama, stories, and art and crafts, and numerous photocopiable pages. (ISBN 0 19 437209 X)

Video, by Richard Cooper, Mike Lavery, and Mario Rinvolucri—video watching and making tasks involving the language of perception, observation, and argumentation. (ISBN 0 19 437192 6)

Vocabulary, by John Morgan and Mario Rinvolucri—a wide variety of communicative activities for teaching new words to learners of any foreign language. (ISBN 437091 7)

Writing, by Tricia Hedge—presents a wide range of writing tasks to improve learners' 'authoring' and 'crafting' skills, as well as guidance on student difficulties with writing. (ISBN 0 19 437098 4)

Young Learners, by Sarah Phillips—advice, ideas, and photocopiable materials for a wide variety of language activities, including arts and crafts, games, storytelling, poems, and songs. (ISBN 0 19 437195 6)

Oxford University Press
English Language Teaching Division

Dear Teacher

We would like your views on how best to develop the *Resource Books for Teachers* series. We would be very grateful if you could fill in this questionnaire and return it to the address at the bottom. We are offering a free OUP wallchart to everyone who returns this form, and ten free Resource Books for the most useful replies received every month.

About yourself

Your name _____

Address_____

_____

_____

Are you: ☐ A teacher?   ☐ A teacher trainer?   ☐ A trainee teacher?

Other? (Please specify) _____

What type of establishment do you work in? _____

What age are your students?   ☐ 3–6   ☐ 6–12   ☐ 12–17   ☐ 18+

How many students per class?   ☐ under 15   ☐ 15–30   ☐ over 30

Which teachers' resource book(s) do you use most (from any publisher)?

_____

Which topic(s) would you most like to have covered in a Resource Book for Teachers?

_____

_____

About *Creating Stories with Children*

Do you read the Introduction? Yes/No

Do you find it useful? Why? _____

Which activities do you find most useful? Why?

_____

_____

Is there anything you **don't** like about the book? _____

_____

We would like your opinion on the size of this book.

Which size do you prefer? ☐ This size   ☐ Don't mind

☐ Other? (Please specify) _____

Do you think that size is best for: ☐ Primary teachers?   ☐ Secondary?   ☐ Adult?

Do you photocopy the worksheets?   Yes/No

Any other comments? (*You can continue your comments on a separate sheet if you wish.*)

_____

_____

Please send your reply to:
Julia Sallabank
Senior Editor, ELT
Oxford University Press
Great Clarendon Street
Oxford
OX2 6DP
UK

Thank you very much for taking the time to answer this questionnaire.

Which wallchart would you prefer?

☐ Map of the UK and world   ☐ The zany zoo (primary)

☐ Map of the USA   ☐ Town scene with worksheets (primary)

☐ English sounds (IPA symbols)

Which Resource Book for Teachers would you prefer? (See the list on the previous two pages.)

Photocopiable © Oxford University Press